BLACK MILLENNIALS & the CHURCH

Meet Me Where I Am

Joshua L. Mitchell

Foreword by Brianna K. Parker

JUDSON PRESS
PUBLISHERS SINCE 1824

Join our mailing list for updates and special offers.
www.judsonpress.com/mailing_list.cfm

Interior design by Beth Oberholtzer.
Cover design by Lisa Delgado Design.

Library of Congress Cataloging-in-Publication Data

Names: Mitchell, Joshua, 1955– author.
Title: Black millennials and the church : meet me where I am / Joshua L. Mitchell.
Description: First [edition]. | Valley Forge : Judson Press, 2018. | Includes bibliographical references.
Identifiers: LCCN 2017025703 (print) | LCCN 2017047352 (ebook) | ISBN 9780817081805 (ebook) | ISBN 9780817017897 (pbk. : alk. paper)
Subjects: LCSH: Bible. Matthew, XIV—Criticism, interpretation, etc. | African Americans—Religion. | African American churches. | Church work with African Americans. | Generation Y—Religious life.
Classification: LCC BS2575.52 (ebook) | LCC BS2575.52 .M58 2018 (print) | DDC 259/.2508996073—dc23
LC record available at https://lccn.loc.gov/2017025703

Printed in the U.S.A.
Second printing, 2019.

Contents

Foreword

I have known Dr. Joshua Mitchell for several years as a colleague and peer. Our time at Virginia Union University formed a bond between us as scholars pursuing culturally relevant work. I have worked with Mitchell on national platforms and witnessed his investment and innovation with Millennials in Houston. As he finished his doctoral work, I was encouraged to see him honing a specialization and clearly defined work around Christian education and discipleship as it relates to black Millennials—a severely underexplored area of practical theology. At a time when few resources are created for the black church, there are far fewer who are concerned with black Millennials. The deficit in this area causes a continuation in a gap that is implosive and destructive to the church.

At a time when Millennials are the buzzword, the excitement around this generation often stops at monetary gain and pastoral bragging rights. "Targeting" Millennials is pervasive in the culture. Everyone wants to know how to attract Millennials for the sake of increasing revenue. From churches to retailers, organizations want to "sell" to Millennials—although no one seems to be able to reciprocate by buying into the unique contributions Millennials bring to the world. As a researcher and consultant, I begin with refusing to create or share gimmicks. I am most pleased to say Dr. Mitchell has not created a book of gimmicks to manipulate Millennials. While most are attempting to tame the monster, he is amplifying the voice of Millennials themselves by sharing their stories for the sake of empowering and equipping our generation.

Not only is work on black Millennials unique and most honestly neglected, a resource allowing black Millennials to read the work of other black Millennials is premier. As a true Millennial himself, Mitchell has created a work that is attractive to other Millennials while including insights and practical tools for older generations of church leaders to implement.

It is imperative that anyone attempting to illuminate the complexities, desires, and systemic barriers of Millennials approach that work with sincerity and courage. Mitchell walks the fine line of exposing the flaws and negligence of the church while encouraging and uplifting the church, leaving congregations with a hope for the future. He does not sanitize the voice of our generation, nor negate the experience of the black church.

Churches and pastors will benefit from the stories shared by black Millennials in this volume. The anonymity used to tell the church's story without embarrassment allows for mutual understanding and exposure. Today, intergenerational conversations are loaded too often with blame and indictments based on feelings and little focus on the goal. The goal is to enhance and empower not just the narrative of the black church but to perfect its humanity, integrity, and engagement in ways that allow progress and hospitality in the world. Mitchell writes toward the goal of a healthy, intergenerational church inspired by the work of all and enhanced by the gifts of the body as a whole through Christian education and cultural progression.

It is my hope that this book will begin a conversation between pastors, staff, congregations, and scholars that produces space for change. It is my prayer that such conversation will transform the church and create spaces where Millennials have not merely a lone voice or token seat at the table, but real stock in the success and longevity of the black church as an institution, community, and incubator for global solutions.

Rev. Dr. Brianna K. Parker
Founding Curator, Black Millennial Cafe

Acknowledgments

The older I get, the more I realize the major roles that others play in my life's accomplishments. My pastor often reminds our congregation, "There is no such thing as a self-made man or woman!" I know that this project would not have happened without a "great cloud of witnesses" who have supported and helped me along the way.

I want to begin with thanksgiving for the incredible ways that God has spared my life and allowed me to be an instrument for God's glory all around the world. I also thank God for my incredible wife, Dr. Lori K. Mitchell, who continues to provide me with both the space and support to do the things that I believe God is calling me to do. You are my best friend, my cheerleader, my sounding board, and sometimes my copyeditor, and I am grateful for all that you have meant in my life and ministry.

As a child, I had many big dreams (including writing books), and I am grateful to God and to my family, my village, my tribe who made me believe that I could achieve those dreams. I thank God for Pastor Marlow L. Mitchell and Lady Pamela D. Mitchell, who are the best parents a young man could ask for. The older I get, the more I appreciate your love, sacrifice, and commitment to ensuring I knew the Lord from my youth, and I thank God always for blessing me to be born into your union. To my ride-or-die little sister, Imani D. Mitchell, I appreciate your listening ear; your ambition to continue to climb to higher heights makes me want to stay on the grind. A special thanks to my aunt Dr. Sharon Moss, who suffered my research-oriented questions; to my grandmother Alma Moss, who never hesitated to correct my English (and look who grew up to be an author!); and to my grandmother Robertha Mitchell, whose prayers and mac and cheese got a brother through! Uncle B, Uncle Raymond, Aunt Eunice, Aunt Angie, Auntie Dr. Juanita Brower, Aunt Debra, Tia, Ray, Gracie, Ramon, Lenny, Al, Vasiliki, BJ—I love and appreciate you all.

I've been blessed with great brothers and accountability partners who would not allow me to quit when the writing process got too hard. Dr. Eric Gill, Rev. Stephen Artis, Rev. Sammie Dow, Rev. Michael Chandler, Rev. O. Chris Buckner, Rev. Melech Thomas, Rev. Corey Gibson, Rev. Michael Moore, Rev. Samuel Burris, Rev. Stephen Dickerson, and Rev. Trey Campbell—I thank you, brothers. I'm grateful to my "day one" STVU sisters—Dr. Brandi Galloway, Rev. Lacette Cross, Rev. Sabrina Dent, Rev. Christy Simmons, Rev. Litticia Clay Crawley, Rev. Lessie Alcin, and Rev. Kaiya Jennings, who continue to inspire and encourage me. To my "Godfathers in the Gospel," Dr. Joseph W. Daniels and Rev. Timothy Warner, thank you for all you have done in my formation process.

The many brothers and sisters of Alpha Nu Omega, Inc. (special shout-outs to Darren, Marcel, and Chris), and the brothers of Alpha Phi Alpha Fraternity, Inc., were instrumental in helping to promote the study. During my freshmen year at Howard I connected with a cohort of Laureate Scholars ("The Brothern") with whom I share a livelong brotherhood, and we have pushed each other to greatness since. This book is made with your love and support.

I have been propelled academically by two wonderful institutions of higher learning. I am forever grateful to my alma mater, Howard University, and specifically to Dr. Audrey Byrd and the Annenberg Honors program for helping me to understand the research process as an undergraduate student. I will never forget Dr. Chuka Onwumechili, who was the first professor to tell me I had what it took to complete doctoral work, and I rode those words of affirmation to the completion of my degree and the genesis of this book. To the bedrock of my theological formation, Virginia Union University, where I spent six years of study for my masters and doctorate—I will forever love and support you. I am grateful to Dr. Alison Gise-Johnson for taking a chance on a young man and for my advisor and mentor, Dr. James Henry Harris, for guiding me through the research process. To my "prophyte" in this work around Black Millennials and Faith at STVU, Rev. Dr. Brianna Parker, I am grateful for your friendship, for your encouragement to join the doctoral program, and for the many ways your groundbreaking work through Black Millennial Café informs my own. My doctoral classmates—better known as Nexus—continuously supported me in this work and I love you all for pushing me to give birth to this book.

This book and the findings of my research study that support it would still be a dream if not for the support and participation of the fantastic members of Wheeler Avenue Baptist Church in Houston, Texas. I am so grateful to our senior pastor, Dr. Marcus D. Cosby, for supporting me in this work and for allowing me to turn the church into my mad scientist lab for a little while. I have been blessed with the opportunity to serve some incredible high schoolers, college students, and young adults at Wheeler, many of whom participated in focus groups and surveys, and I love each of you for your contributions to this work. To "The Brook" and my M6:33 family, all of this was sparked by our time together (what you say?) and you have taught me more than any book or quantitative data analysis could have. I love you all to life. To Pastor Andrew W. Berry II, Pastor Linda Stevens, and the youth and young adults I've served at Greater Barbours Chapel, New Life Empowerment Temple, and Rising Sun Baptist Church—you all have made invaluable contributions to this work.

In my estimation, the "soul" of the book comes from the interviews of the Millennials who are featured in our "Valuable Voices" sections. Not everyone who participated desired to have their real names used in the book, but I am beyond grateful to Danielle F., Rev. B. Jerrad, Rev. Joseph A. C. Smith, Kay Williams, Nichole, Peyton Morris, Rev. Sammie J. Dow, Rev. Verdell

A. Wright, Rev. Dr. Neichelle R. Guidry, Empress Aset Sekhmet Maut, Rev. Chelir Grady, and Rev. Candace Simpson for your invaluable contributions to this project. I love and appreciate you all.

Finally, to the Judson Press family—thank you for taking a chance on a young, first-time author with a vision to help the church. I appreciate this opportunity more than you know. I am grateful for the guidance of Dr. Adam Bond and Rev. Rebecca Irwin-Diehl in this process, from proposal to publication, and I look forward to seeing great fruit from this adventure together.

Where Do We Begin?

Ladies and gentlemen, welcome to "Millennial Mania!" It is difficult for me to pinpoint the exact date or time when it happened, but somewhere near the mid-2010s, organizations around the country became obsessed with understanding the so-called Millennial generation and its impending impact on various segments of society. Today there is no shortage of articles and news updates informing the masses of what Millennials eat, or how Millennials drive, or where Millennials shop (and the list goes on). Eventually the Christian church caught on, realizing that we could not afford to misunderstand what makes this generation of churchgoers and leaders tick, and Christians began to research and write about the intersection of Millennials and Christianity. Authors and researchers such as Thom Rainer, Drew Dyck, and F. Douglas Powe have sought to inform the church of the elements that compel and repel Millennials to the Word and work of the Christian faith.

I stumbled into my work on Millennials through the help of a dear friend, Dr. Brianna Parker, who was beginning her doctoral work at Virginia Union University. In truth, I have been working with members of the Millennial generation since I accepted my call to ministry in 2005, but I originally sought to complete my doctoral work in Homiletics. Encouraged by then-Rev. Parker to consider returning to Virginia Union University to matriculate through their doctoral program, I went into the program hoping to create a new paradigm for preaching—and came out with the research that undergirds the content of this book.

As I began to realize the challenges of my ministry context, it became clear that preaching was not our issue. What we needed to figure out was how to effectively reach, keep, and disciple the black Millennials in our congregations and the surrounding community. The more I reviewed the literature, the more I saw the need for research and writing focused on black Millennials, because the findings and assertions about "all" Millennials and their faith formation did not seem to ring true with what I was experiencing in the African American community and the black church.

Following in the footsteps of Dr. Parker, who created a first-of-its-kind nationwide survey to investigate the intersection of black Millennials and faith, my doctoral project sought to narrow the conversation and its implications for ministry and discipleship within the Christian church. In 2016, I launched a nationwide survey focused on the factors that would increase the willingness of black Millennials to engage in spiritual formation at a local church body. This survey was accompanied by focus groups and interviews with black Millennials who were a part of the faith and with others who had once been a part of the Christian faith but no longer identified with Christianity. Ultimately more than 600 black Millennials were surveyed or interviewed, and the data and insights resulting from that research inform the claims that will be made throughout this book.

To be sure, this book is not a work full of facts and figures. Most of the percentages and ratios that come out of my study will not appear at all in this book. What is more important to me is that readers walk away with what the numbers mean, and that they are afforded an opportunity to hear from Millennial leaders in various spaces who can help congregations ask critical questions around their proclamation, programming, and priorities. To be clear, not everything presented in the book aligns with my own theological framework, but what is presented will represent the authentic voices of the black Millennials who participated and provided their voices to the research and writing process.

CHAPTER ONE

Good Grief

"After he had dismissed
them, he went up on a
mountainside by himself
to pray. Later that night,
he was there alone."

MATTHEW 14:23

Meet Pastor Smith. Pastor Smith is the eighth senior pastor to serve in the 85-year history of Doing the Best We Can Baptist Church in Anywhere, USA. The church was founded during the height of the Civil Rights movement and soon became the pillar of the local African American community. It developed a reputation for being a church where one could count on hearing powerful preaching and great music each week. The church was also known for being actively engaged in the struggle for important policy reform and community services. The powerful preaching of the church's fourth pastor, Dr. Great-Voice, attracted incredible crowds and compelled the congregation to build its current, larger edifice in the heart of the city. For decades, Sunday morning worship services were standing-room-only affairs as every pew on the floor and balcony teemed with young families who were enthused about their church and were actively participating in the life and ministry of the congregation.

Unfortunately, this is not the Doing the Best We Can Baptist Church that Pastor Smith inherited. While the young people who flooded the pews during the era of Pastor Great-Voice are still members of the church, they have now transitioned into "senior saint" status and the average age of the membership has shifted to 63 years old. The congregation has sought to maintain many of the traditions and physical structures of the church's heyday, but in many ways it is a completely different church. The sanctuary is still adorned with incredible stained-glass windows depicting various awe-inspiring biblical stories, yet the number of people gathered in the sanctuary each Sunday to admire the glass images has drastically decreased. In the most recent church business meeting, Pastor Smith mentioned the need for the congregation to be intentional and prayerful about attracting younger members, but he is fearful that the closure of the church building is only a matter of time. At the conclusion of this week's Wednesday night Bible study class, Pastor Smith took a long look at the faithful gathering of nearly 25 senior citizens and his wife and children in the first row. Pastor Smith looked out onto the rows of empty pews and sighed deeply in frustration. *Something has got to give,* he thought. *This place is becoming a "ghost town."*

Many pastors and church leaders of black congregations in the twenty-first century can identify all too well with the frustrations of Pastor Smith (maybe even more than our pride will allow us to admit). Countless churches around the country that once stood as powerful pillars in their respective communities are seeing faithful parishioners age into retirement without a steady influx of young adults to carry the torch for the church into future decades.

By all accounts this generation of young adults known as the *Millennials* (individuals born between 1982 and 2000) are increasingly disinterested in traditional church experiences. Despite our best programming and outreach efforts many churches have been unable to attract, retain, and spiritually develop a substantial number of this generation. As a result, church leaders such as Pastor Smith are not just *frustrated* with the state of their congregations but they find themselves in a state of bereavement. Many pastors and congregational leaders are grieving the perceived loss of the church's youth, vitality, and possibly even the church's relevance in a strange new digital world. For many congregations who are having trouble attracting and developing this next generation of the church, their primary concern comes down to some form of this critically relevant question: *Can our church survive and thrive for the next 60 years, or have we already become "the walking dead"?*

Mountainside Moments

This idea of "the walking dead" is a central theme in the Gospel of Matthew's story of Jesus walking on water. The story begins in Matthew 14:22 as Jesus made his disciples get into a boat and travel to "the other side" of the lake following a long day of ministry. As they sailed away, Jesus traveled alone to the side of a mountain for a time of prayer. If we read the story in context, we find that Jesus' mountainside moment was not simply designed to recharge after a long day of ministry, but it also gave him time and space alone to *grieve*. Earlier in the fourteenth chapter of Matthew's Gospel, Jesus received news that his cousin, John the Baptist, had been killed. But before Jesus had the opportunity to be alone with his thoughts, the demands of the people who followed him prevented him from immediately dealing with his own concerns and hurts. (Does any of this sound familiar?) A few healings, exorcisms, and thousands of fish sandwiches later, and Jesus finally was alone on the mountainside to grieve what he had lost.

In many ways this book is designed to help pastors and church leaders who find themselves in the midst of "mountainside moments." These are not to be confused with "mountain-*top* moments"—those moments in ministry when we feel we are operating at our best, hearing the applause of the masses, and happy about all the *good* things that God is doing through us and for us. Mountainside moments are periods of time when we reflect upon the *grief* that has gripped us in the course of our ministry work. As congregations seeking to engage and develop this generation of young adults face inevitable challenges, many leaders are experiencing one of two kinds of grief.[1]

There are some who are experiencing a form of conventional grief, the normal process of mourning after losing something important to us. We may be grieving the loss of the booming youth group or young adult ministry that the church was known for in previous decades. Normally this grief manifests itself in variations of the following chorus reverberating around the church: *When Pastor Tiffany was here, we had young people everywhere!*

Other church leaders are experiencing what is called *anticipatory grief.* "Anticipatory grief is mourning that occurs when a family is *expecting* a death."[2] While some of us may not openly admit it, we are frightened by the lack of young adult participation in our churches. As we watch the current stakeholders of our congregations continue to age, we face a scary reality—a reality that could spell the slow death of many of our local assemblies. The fear and sorrow that accompanies this reality connects many leaders with Jesus' position in Matthew 14. We find ourselves tired and possibly alone on the mountain, evaluating how our losses (or potential losses) will affect us and those whom we are called to serve.

In both types of grief, taking time for mountainside moments is necessary and transformative. While the grief process can be grueling and terrible for our egos, I would argue that this grief is actually *good grief.* It points to a true care and concern for the life of the congregations we are called to serve and the souls of a generation we seek to see saved. Moreover, acknowledging our grief and concerns for our churches refocuses us so that we can clearly see where we need to go and what we need to do next.

Consider the Scripture story again. It is *after* Jesus takes the time to grieve, pray, and evaluate on the mountainside that he is able to turn and clearly see the distress of his young disciples being tossed by the violent waves of the lake. That clarity sets in motion an encounter between Jesus and the disciples that ushers in the dawn of new possibilities and a deeper awareness of the power and person of Jesus for everyone on board.

Setting the Stage

This book is designed to speak to those who are discerning a call to engage (or reengage) and spiritually develop this current generation of young adults, but who may be unclear on where to start. Stylistically, this book is crafted to make the content easily accessible to a variety of ministry leaders. Senior pastors, denominational leaders, Sunday school teachers, and small group leaders alike can benefit from the content in the pages to come. Many churches have very few young adults within the congregation; others have a congregation overflowing with Millennials, but those young adults are disengaged in discipleship development outside of the Sunday morning worship experience. Whichever may be the case in your faith community, this work seeks to provide practical strategies to attract, retain, and ultimately disciple this unique generation of young people who will be needed to carry the church into the second half of the twenty-first century. The purpose of this book is not to teach you how to grow a megachurch overflowing with Millennials (read 1 Corinthians 3:7 on that subject), but rather to help provide church leaders in any congregation with an understanding of who these young people are and the principles needed to better engage them and grow them into men and women in the image and likeness of Jesus Christ.

This book is especially useful for congregations and organizations seeking to minister primarily to black Millennials. The bulk of the content is birthed out of my own doctoral research and the subsequent consulting I've done with congregations hoping to attract, retain, and prayerfully disciple black Millennials. As both a church leader and a Millennial leader myself who is responsible for shepherding young people of my own generation, I quickly realized that this generation of young adults has unique spiritual outlooks, assumptions, family upbringings, cultural norms, and technological advances that require me to approach ministry and outreach efforts differently than my parents generation did. Yet I found that most of the research and books surrounding

Millennials and the Christian church are centered around the norms and characteristics of white Millennials—norms and characteristics that are often very different from their black and brown counterparts in African American and Latino communities. As a product and pastoral leader of the black church, it is important for me to get a better understanding of the unique nuances and needs of black Millennials, and the research that birthed this book was itself born from this ongoing search.

The claims of this book are based primarily on the results of my nationwide survey called *Black Millennials and Discipleship,* and they are enhanced by additional information garnered from several interviews and focus groups. More than 600 black Millennials from around the United States and U.S. Virgin Islands shared their stories and perspectives through our study, and churches seeking to minister to black Millennials will greatly benefit from their insights.

Not Just Hearers of the Word

The goal of this book is to provide pastors and church leaders with not just facts and figures, but to provide practical principles that can be applied within your context today. I have found that the best way to localize the principles of this book for individual congregations and organizations is to facilitate pointed dialogue around each key idea. To this end, each chapter will end with a brief section called "Walking on Water." In those sections, readers will be provided with discussion questions that will help connect the material in the chapter to the unique makeup of your congregation or organization. While these discussion questions can be answered by individual readers, it is more beneficial for a congregation or leadership team to engage the material in the book as a group. Working through the book as a team will expand the conversation, expose your ministry "blind spots," and broaden the realm of possible solutions.

Throughout the book, readers will also find sidebars designated "Valuable Voices"—excerpts from interviews with individual Millennials who have expertise or experience in the various areas of conversation throughout the book. These interviews may provide the most helpful information of all, helping give voice and life to the findings of the study. In the end, the purpose of the book is not to provide pastors and church leaders with statistics, data, and knowledge for knowledge's sake, but to equip congregations prayerfully to walk out onto the waters of new possibility and engage this generation in new and exciting ways!

Bid Me to Come

As Jesus came toward the boat in Matthew 14, the disciples saw him as a "ghost," something that was once alive but is now dead. In many ways the disciples' view of Jesus is consistent with the way black Millennials view the traditions, programming, and teachings of the Christian church. Yet the Scripture text is also very encouraging, as it teaches us that there are people—specifically, some black Millennials—who are still willing to engage those whom others will label as "dead."

Over the course of this book, we will correlate the principles of the story in Matthew 14 to the lessons those willing black Millennials are teaching us about how to engage and develop them as strong disciples of Jesus Christ through the ministries of our congregations. Like most water-walking experiences, the process of engagement can cause fear and discomfort. At times we may even feel like we are drowning in our attempts to connect, but the results that our efforts will yield for our congregations and the kingdom of God are well worth the attempts. If you are up for the challenge of growing a new generation of young disciples of Christ, it's time to grab a poncho and some rain boots, and meet me out on the sea with Jesus. There's a storm to be tamed and some young disciples to be engaged!

VALUABLE VOICES

Featured Millennial: Danielle F., age 27, Acquisitions Specialist, U.S. Government

On her religious upbringing . . .

My religious upbringing was in a traditional Baptist church. The Bible and the biblical teaching—that was definitely taught to me, but I don't feel like it was forced upon me. I think that I had a very busy and active church life. We were probably in church three to four days out of any given week. My church was not close by my hometown, so we had to travel.

I spent a lot of time in the church. I spent a lot of time traveling to and from the church, and therefore spent significant time away from friends and any other activities that I thought I might've wanted to participate in. My heavy involvement in the church had its pros and cons, but I still don't feel as if Christ was forced down my throat as maybe one would say because of how often we were there. I think that my parents made sure that the practices of going to church and understanding who God is were there, but they did not force me to accept God. They did not force me to have a relationship with God, but they did make sure that I had a good foundation.

On the benefits of her traditional church upbringing . . .

Most of the benefits I believe I didn't appreciate until later in life. At the time of my upbringing, [I would be] in church all day, four days a week, and [with church] being so far away from home, I don't feel that I had an opportunity to really have a social life. While yes, I had friends at school and things of that sort, those friends were able to enjoy extracurricular activities with one another and went to church together because their churches were closer to the city, while I felt like I lived a double life. I lived in one city and had church friends and family, really a whole additional life, somewhere else. I don't think I appreciated that then, and still would probably do it differently now. That was a trial for me growing up.

The church in and of itself, however, was awesome. I learned discipline. While I feel like I had a lot of good, wise people involved in my rearing, the wiser and older senior members of the church who were there made sure that there was no disruption in the church. We understood the decorum; we understood what decency and order were all about. I actually loved my church growing up. There were a lot of young people in church, so I felt like I had a little family that I got to grow up with. But unfortunately, as time went on everybody had to go and live their own lives and so I don't really feel that same connection in the church anymore.

On how things have changed (or stayed the same) . . .

Obviously some things have shifted. People have grown up; they've gone other places. But one thing I don't care for now is that the church that I grew up in is somewhat in the same place practice-wise that it was in when I was there. It hasn't really moved with the times. Not that the content in preaching should move, but how we worship, how we reach out to others with the gospel—for those whom we need to reach out to who are not a part of the Body—how we spread the gospel, I don't think that the church has adapted to that.

So it really can't speak to me and things that I'm going through today, as a young adult, as a 27-year-old, soon to be 30-year-old, soon to be possibly married, with kids. I don't feel that it is nurturing me in what I'm currently going through at this stage in my life. The membership is a lot older. They don't seem to have that middle ground. There's a big generational gap there that I think encompasses a lot of missing elements to the worship experience that now I'm looking for at other churches.

What she is looking for in a church in her adult years . . .

Some of the elements I'm looking for . . . [At] this point in my life, I'm looking for a strong youth and young adult ministry with people being within the age group of, like, 21 to 39. I think that's important to have a ministry for that age group specifically, because there are certain things that you deal with in that middle ground that just are not being addressed.

For example, when you're a child you get poured into. You get put on the church's choir, you become a part of the Junior Usher Board, so you get taught the foundation. But now, in real adult life, we're missing the application portion. Those who poured into us as children are not really still pouring into us as young adults anymore. They think that that nourishment in those teachings is supposed to automatically transfer now that we're out of their homes, and that's not necessarily the case.

So there's a big gap, in terms of young adults being taught, nourished, guided in the church, and the church has to continue to, in some ways, "market" to that age group. Why should I come to church before taking a day of rest because I've been working all week? Why should I come and be a part of this ministry when really I need to be going and doing this over here? I want to live my life; I want to do something different. What is it about the church that is drawing me in, as opposed to shutting me out, because of my youth?

I think that oftentimes we're also missing the appreciation of what young adults can bring. Sometimes I feel like our ideas and our talents are not really being utilized and sought after, so that is another way that you can be pushed away from the church. People talk about how "we are the future" when really we are *the today*. So sometimes I think it's imperative that they incorporate the young adults in the religious experience, incorporate the young adults into the business of the church, and not just give it to those who've been there for years and years and years, because there are things that we can bring to the space that you won't bring to us. That's a mistake.

In the church that I grew up in, we're lacking modernization. We're lacking the technology and those things that kind of are appealing to us today. Consider your social media. If I can't get to the church, can I stream it? If I can't get to the church, can I give online? If I can't get to the church, what's going on? I live out of town now and my home church is hours away, but I might still want to know what some of the events are. And I would normally find things like that out based off of their Instagram page or Facebook, but they don't have that. So I have a disconnect from that church while I'm away. I don't too much care for that, because I'm now going to a new church, and that church, no matter where I am, I'm always connected to it. No matter where I am, I can hear the sermon from that week. I can hear the Bible studies from that week. I can hear sermons and Bible studies from months ago. I can virtually ask them to be part of the prayer list. I can give my tithes and offerings, to specify where I want it to go to, and make sure that my stuff is tracking. All of that is important to a young adult who's always on the move, who wants to take vacations, who has to work all the time. The accessibility of the church, not just being a physical location, is key to me. That's something that I'm looking for as well.

Walking on Water

1. What is your current congregational makeup?

2. In what ways are you experiencing a conventional or anticipatory grief surrounding your church or organization's engagement with young adults? What are your fears and concerns for the future?

3. Who are the leaders within your church or organization that may also need to engage this content in community with you?

NOTES

1. Lynn Eldridge, "Understanding Anticipatory Grief: Why Am I Already Grieving?" last modified July 27, 2017, https://www.verywell.com/understanding-anticipatory-grief-and-symptoms-2248855.

2. Medicine Net Corporation, "Medical Definition of Anticipatory Grief," accessed April 7, 2017, http://www.medicinenet.com/script/main/art.asp?articlekey=26258.

CHAPTER TWO

"And I Tell You That You Are Peter"

"'And I tell you that you are Peter, and on this rock I will build my church, and the gates of Hades will not overcome it.'"

MATTHEW 16:18

Before we dive into the dance between Jesus and Peter on the lake, it is important to note the relationship that has developed between Peter and Jesus. The Gospel writers identify Peter as the first disciple called by Jesus and beckoned to learn from Jesus. They travel and dine together, they work in ministry together, and over time, Peter gleans enough from Jesus to be left in charge of the movement when Jesus ascends into Heaven. However, as Peter is getting to know Jesus, Jesus is also paying close attention to Peter—learning his patterns and tendencies and seeing future possibilities that Peter does not always see in himself. It is this relationship, this mutual knowledge of each other, which ultimately sets the stage for Peter to trust Jesus by engaging him on the lake in Matthew 14.

This same mutual knowledge and understanding of one another must also exist between the Christian church and the black Millennials we hope will engage us on the waters of spiritual formation. Often I find that churches desire who they call black "Millenniums" to be a part of their fellowship, but know little to nothing about who these young adults are or what makes them tick. This is unfortunate because, in contrast, black Millennials know *a lot* about the church.

Many black Millennials have had some connection with the Christian church—either by being reared in the life of a congregation or by living with grandparents or loved ones who proclaimed faith in Christ. They've also been overly exposed to the negative aspects of the church—with the scandals and shortcomings of congregations becoming all-too-frequent launching pads for blog posts, Twitter wars, and television series. As a result, long before they darken the doors of a local place of worship, many black Millennials have preconceived notions of the Christian church that the church must contend with—in the same way that many older members of congregations have preconceived notions of who these Millennials are.

In this chapter, I will seek to provide a snapshot of this Millennial generation, referring to some of the major characteristics of the generation as a whole and then relying on the study data to paint a more specific picture of black Millennials. This chapter is by no means exhaustive, but I hope that it will provide a general idea of what fuels this generation of "Peters" that our congregations seek to engage.

Millennials 101

Lesson number one: not every young adult is a Millennial, and not every Millennial is a young adult. Often I hear the "Millennial" tag thrown around to identify a life stage called "young adult," based on an age range of 18 to 35 years old (which is a "moving target" as time passes), as opposed to a specific generational cohort bound by specific birthdates. Millennials are the latter, a cohort originally defined by generational theorists William Strauss and Neil Howe[1] as the U.S. generation of persons born between 1982 and 2000. To be sure, there are other theorists and writers who utilize different birth years to frame the generation and some researchers have alternatively labeled Millennials as "Generation Y." However, for the purposes of this book, we will utilize Strauss and Howe's original framework for defining the generation.

With these dates in mind, it is fair to say that at the time of publication for this work, most Millennials are indeed young adults (roughly aged 18 to 36). However, this paradigm will begin to shift as the oldest Millennials approach middle age (their 40s and 50s) and the oldest members of the subsequent generation (so-called Generation Z, born between 2001 and 2020) move into their later years of high school education. Currently, Millennials represent the largest generational cohort in U.S. history. They are even more numerous than Baby Boomers—although sociologists project they may soon be surpassed in size by the emerging Generation Z. The Millennial generation is also the most educated, most racially diverse, and most religiously unaffiliated generation that our nation has ever produced.

Strauss and Howe's *Millennials Rising* is one of the earliest books written about Millennials, published in 2000 while many of the cohort were still developing as children. Paul Taylor's *The Next America*[2] provides extensive data and a profile of Millennials as adults. Published in 2014, Taylor's work utilizes statistical data compiled by the Pew Research Center to help readers understand Millennials in light of the socioeconomic makeup of the three other adult generations living in the U.S. (Generation Xers, Baby Boomers, and the Silent Generation). While Strauss and Howe's work surveyed the Millennial landscape as children, Taylor's work is valuable because it presents a portrait of the Millennial generation after the majority of them have transitioned into adulthood. As such, it becomes a primary source for the exploration of the generation.

In his interpretation of the Pew Research Center data compiled about the four adult generations in the United States, Taylor asserts that the "young and old in America are poles apart. Demographically, politically, economically, socially, and technologically, these generations are more different from each other than at any time in living memory."[3] Taylor's research suggests that Millennials are "liberal, diverse (racially and culturally), tolerant, narcissistic, coddled, respectful, confident and broke."[4] While much of Taylor's interest in *The Next America* surrounds the impending political and socioeconomic "showdown" between Millennials and Boomers, he also presents helpful information about Millennials and religion.

Taylor writes, "They have a different view of religion. A third of Millennials are unaffiliated with any religion, compared with 9% of Silents, 15% of Boomers, and 21% of Gen Xers. Millennials are the least religiously connected generation in modern American history."[5] Taylor dedicates an entire chapter of his book to the growing demographic of Millennials who consider themselves unaffiliated with any organized religion—a group Taylor refers to as "Nones" because of their frequent response of "none" when asked about their religious affiliation in research surveys. His profile on this unaffiliated demographic is telling. Millennials identify as politically "liberal," and while these so-called Nones are not connected to any organized religion, more than two-thirds of unaffiliated Millennials still believe in the existence of God.[6]

Taylor presents three leading interpretations for the rise of religiously unaffiliated Millennials. The first theory surrounds political backlash, claiming many "have turned away from organized religion because they perceive it as deeply entangled with conservative politics and do not want to have any association with it."[7] The second theory Taylor discusses identifies a correlation between the delay in marriage for Millennials and religious affiliation, citing a Pew Research Center poll showing "that among adults under 30, the married are more likely than the unmarried to have a religious affiliation."[8] Third, Taylor cites sociologists such as Robert Putnam who assert that "the growth of the religious 'nones' is just one manifestation of much broader social disengagement."[9]

Taylor's work is most helpful in his identification and subsequent discussion of Millennials as "digital natives." Taylor defines digital natives as members "of the first generation in history for whom digital technology platforms are the essential mediators of social life and information acquisition."[10] As Taylor notes, Millennials' relationship with digital technology "has played a fundamental role in shaping the nature of their friendships, the structure of their social networks, the way they learn, their provision and acceptance of social support, the way they interact with groups and institutions, their posture towards the wider world, and the way they allocate their time."[11]

It is worth noting that Taylor's "digital natives" conversation provides helpful perspective for organizations seeking to educate Millennials, including the church. Teaching paradigms dependent on oral presentations and lectures (such as sermons and didactic Bible study) can be a barrier for a Millennial audience socialized to receive essential information through digital technology. Any attempts to reengage black Millennials in the teaching ministries of our local congregations must consider their relationship to digital technology.

F. Douglas Powe and Ministry to Black Millennials

As I combed through the existing literature in preparation for my study, it was difficult to find specific books and articles that highlighted the nuances of the black members of the Millennial cohort. While there were many things that the generation had in common across racial demographics, my gut told me that things weren't exactly the same for Millennials of color. One of the most helpful resources I discovered in this area was the work of F. Douglas Powe Jr.

In a field of study that has produced very little on the nuances of the African American Millennial experience and their implications for churches seeking to foster the spiritual formation process among this generation, F. Douglas Powe Jr.'s *New Wine, New Wineskins*[12] becomes an important primary source. F. Douglas Powe Jr., who earned his PhD in Systematic Theology and serves as the James C. Logan Professor of Evangelism and Professor of

Urban Ministry and the Associate Director of the Center for Missional Church at Wesley Theological Seminary, provides the first sustained treatment on how the black church can reach African American Millennials. Powe begins his book with a profile of the four current American generational categories as outlined in Strauss and Howe's seminal work *Generations* and their subsequent *Millennials Rising* (Silents, Boomers, Gen Xers, and Millennials). Expanding on their work, Powe "redefines these categories to address the generational shifts within the African American community."[13] Redefining black Millennials as the "Hip Hop generation" born between 1981 and 2000, Powe paints black Millennials as capitalistic, relationally driven, educationally split by class divisions, perceived as politically unimportant, and technologically savvy (and dependent).

Powe's work is helpful because of his attention to the trends and needs of black Millennials in the Christian church. While discussing the Hip Hop generation's impact on the church, Powe writes, "This generation does shift the African American Christian landscape, because many are more comfortable in mega congregations that mimic a celebrity culture. These congregations tend to be higher tech and make use of various media formats that have become normative for this generation."[14] Powe also reviews the changes in black Millennials' relationship and expectations of their preacher/pastor. Powe writes, "One of the attractions of these congregations is the well-known senior pastor. The Hip Hop generation does not need to know the pastor personally, but must feel connected to the pastor and church. This can happen via social networks or based upon the pastor's status."[15]

Powe's directive to congregations seeking to reach black Millennials is that "it is time to rethink church for post–civil rights generations."[16] For Powe, this includes rethinking (if not dismissing) several assumptions that African American congregations have operated from for many generations, including "the old wineskin mentality of African American congregations being the epicenter in the community, shaping the reality of the community, and having the right vision for the community."[17] The new wineskin that Powe suggests is an "ecclesiology that is inclusive of the voices of the post–civil rights generations by rethinking concepts like space, collaboration, and empowerment."[18] In short, Powe argues that reaching black Millennials will require finding spaces outside the church to create sanctuary; increasing collaboration across generations within the church; partnering with institutions outside the church; and becoming open to the Spirit's desire and ability to bridge the communication gap between the language of the Millennials and the older generations.[19]

One major strength of Powe's work is the theological model that grounds his suggestions to African American congregations seeking to reach black Millennials. As Powe calls for black congregations to become missional regarding reaching black Millennials, he advances a Trinitarian pattern and model that is grounded in an understanding of the gospel and the Holy Spirit. According to Powe,

> Congregations that can maintain a solid theological grounding while rethinking the way the gospel is embodied will be vital. Missional congregations are committed to the gospel and to helping connect others to the gospel. Missional congregations are willing to rethink the way they make space for others, collaborate on the embodiment of the gospel and seek a holistic understanding of the Spirit.[20]

Powe's theological foundation in his advancement of ideas for reaching black Millennials is refreshing. He does not simply provide "best practices" but stresses the importance of the participation of the Spirit.

Black Millennials: Family Dynamics, Life Markers, Pop Culture, and Ministry

My nationwide survey sought to dig a little deeper into demographical nuances of black Millennials. From our survey data we were able to identify distinctive characteristics about black Millennials that may be important in a congregation's understanding of the generation. While I will not attempt to provide an extensive look at all of the statistics and figures compiled from our study, I will briefly highlight a few important themes in the areas of family dynamics, life markers, popular culture experienced through music and media, and ministry preferences.

Family Dynamics

The notion of family is both central and diverse for black Millennials. This is the generation that grew up watching black families modeled in prime time through shows such as *Family Matters* and *The Fresh Prince of Bel-Air*, although many black Millennials did not grow up in the "traditional" two-parent household depicted in those television series. Nearly 40 percent of the black Millennials in our study were raised by a single parent, and the theme of fatherlessness frequently recurs in the stories of many of the black Millennials we interviewed.

Like many of their white generational cohorts, a great number of black Millennials are still living at home. Nearly one-third of black Millennials reported living with at least one parent, while others are living with friends and roommates. Relationally, most black Millennials identify as single/never married, consistent with a larger generational trend of Millennials getting married much later than previous generations.

Significant Life Markers

When Strauss and Howe published *Millennials Rising* in 2000, they suggested that the Columbine shooting would serve as a primary life marker for the Millennial generation. This was not the case for black Millennials. Through our study, black Millennials identified three national events as generational life markers.

The first event was the terrorist attacks on September 11, 2001, most significantly on the World Trade Center in New York. Many of the black Millennials we spoke with could still remember the teacher whose classroom they were sitting in when news of the attacks was first reported. Second among the events of great significance for most black Millennials was the election (and the subsequent reelection) of the first black president, Barack Obama.

Finally, the third most significant life marker for black Millennials was the shooting death of Trayvon Martin. Many point to this event as the "Emmet Till lynching" of their generation, observing that they were compelled into the movement for black lives as a result of the death of Martin and the countless other unarmed black men and women to follow.

Hurricane Katrina, the election of Donald Trump, the Pulse nightclub shooting in Orlando, and the emergence of the Black Lives Matter movement itself were other national events that have shaped the lives and consciousness of this generation.

Millennials, Music, and Media Use

This generation of digital natives has grown up on a steady diet of media consumption that has shaped the way individuals operate in the world as adults. As children, they were reared by television programming including *Rugrats*, *Boy Meets World*, and *Power Rangers*, and as adolescents they grew to enjoy programs such as *Martin*, *Living Single*, and *The Simpsons*. They are also the first generation to grow up with reality television, consuming shows such as MTV's *The Real World* that helped to set the stage for society's reality TV obsession.

Black Millennials reported growing up loving the music of artists such as Michael Jackson, Kirk Franklin, TLC, and Destiny's Child during their childhood, and Usher, Beyoncé, Lil' Wayne, and Jay-Z during their teenage years. Many black Millennials learned the basics of computer programming through the use of high-level Texas Instruments calculators like the popular TI-83 (they could program their own games on it), and these Millennials also grew up during the development of the video game era. Handheld gaming devices, virtual pets, and gaming consoles such as the PlayStation®, Nintendo 64, and Xbox were technological fixtures in the homes of black Millennials, who also were a part of the first generation of children and adolescents to have access to cellular phone devices.

Today, the electronic device of choice for black Millennials is the smartphone. These digital natives utilize it for everything—

from engaging in community with peers through social media to arranging transportation through ride-sharing applications such as Lyft and Uber.

Black Millennials and Ministry

Like their white counterparts, although at a slower rate, black Millennials are pulling away from the Christian church and organized religion. However, those who do attend church are relatively active participants in the life of their local congregations. The majority of black Millennials who report being members of a local church also report attending worship on a weekly basis and viewing worship online at least once per month. Two-thirds of black Millennials who are members of churches are active participants in at least one of the church's ministries, and more than 70 percent report being regular tithers in the church.

Regarding the ministries that are of interest to black Millennials, young adult ministries, worship and arts ministries, and volunteering with youth ministries are the most popular, while black Millennials reported the least amount of interest in singles ministries, men's ministries, and women's ministries. For black Millennials, the preaching and presence of the senior pastor, the music ministry, and the character of the people who make up a particular congregation are the most important factors in choosing to fellowship with a church. Conversely, the individual's own family history with a church, the standard dress code and attire of a local body, and the size of a congregation were *not* important factors for black Millennials in picking a church for their spiritual formation process.

Black Millennials still believe in the value of Christian education, even when they are not present in the sanctuary to receive it. More than 80 percent of black Millennials who are members of local churches believe that participating in Bible study, Sunday school, and other teaching ministries at their churches is essential to their spiritual development—although nearly half of black Millennial church members reported not attending any of these offerings on a regular basis. (We will discuss in later chapters that the lack of attendance in the teaching ministries of the church is not an indication of a lack of interest in spiritual formation, but rather reflects challenges in the availability of the content.)

As we return to the story of Jesus and Peter walking on the lake in Matthew 14 and begin to glean direction on how to engage and develop black Millennials in our congregations, it is important to consider these developmental nuances of these modern "Peters" whom we seek to engage. Now that we know a little more about them, let's see if we can get them to step out of their boats.

VALUABLE VOICES

Featured Millennial: Rev. B. Jerrad, age 32, Media specialist and Associate Minister, Houston, TX

Tell us a bit about your upbringing and how you ultimately got so active in the ministry of the Church . . .

I was raised in a single parent home, just me and my mom, but I had my grandparents—my grandmother and grandfather to help raise me. [The single parent upbringing] was consistent in my friend group. If you looked at all of my friends growing up, the majority of us just had our mothers. Dad wasn't around for various [reasons]. Only one of my friends have both of their parents. I grew up watching *Family Matters*, *Amen*, and *Full House* and my grandfather was very instrumental in helping me to learn more about God and church. He was a pastor in the Trinity Gardens area in Houston and it was there that I began to aspire to be like him. One Christmas he bought me a briefcase just like his and from there I really began to imagine working in ministry [vocationally]. I announced my calling at 15 years old. I was entering my sophomore year of high school, and my mother and grandparents helped to raise me and ensure I was active in the church. They taught me right from wrong, they helped me to learn Scripture, I sang in the choir, I worked with the deacons, and everywhere my grandfather went I would tag along. Every convention, every association meeting—if he was going, I wanted to go.

What factored into your decision to leave the church of your family's history and worship/serve elsewhere?

I'm no longer serving in the church where he [my grandfather] pastored, which was our family church, because he was no longer pastoring. . . . I'm no longer there because I felt like I outgrew the church. I wanted more spiritual maturity and I wanted a place where I could get more deeply involved in ministry and in the church.

When I found my current church, I felt the passion and the conviction in the preaching of my new pastor, and I'm volunteering in the Youth Ministry because I've always loved youth. I've been around youth since my teenage years, even as a young preacher. I taught youth Sunday School, I taught Bible study, I preached Youth Sunday every month—so I've been working with youth for my 16 years in ministry.

What would you suggest to local churches seeking to effectively engage black Millennials?

As a whole, church families have to be intentional about bridging the gap between the young and the old, allowing space for the young to get wisdom from the old. And the elders need to also listen to what the young have to say and see if they can incorporate what they have to say into how the church is run so that our local churches don't die out. Moreover, I think Millennials need to cultivate a heart to serve in the church. (That's not normative in our celebrity-driven culture.) Serving is important—there's a blessing attached to it and it feels great to serve God and God's people.

Walking on Water

1. What are some of the things you already knew about black Millennials prior to reading this chapter?

2. What are some of the new insights about black Millennials you now have?

3. How can this information help you as you seek to engage this unique generation?

NOTES

1. William Strauss and Neil Howe, *Millennials Rising: The Next Great Generation* (New York: Vintage Books, 2000), Kindle Edition. Loc. 75.
2. Paul Taylor, *The Next America: Boomers, Millennials, and the Looming Generational Showdown* (New York: Public Affairs, 2014), Kindle Edition.
3. Taylor, Loc. 663.
4. Ibid., Loc. 604.
5. Ibid., Loc. 687.
6. Ibid., Loc. 2535.
7. Ibid., Loc. 2604.
8. Ibid., Loc. 2818.
9. Ibid., Loc. 2618.
10. Ibid., Loc. 2773.
11. Ibid., Loc. 2781.
12. F. Douglas Powe Jr., *New Wine, New Wineskins: How African American Congregations Can Reach New Generations* (Nashville: Abingdon Press, 2012), Kindle Edition.
13. Ibid., Loc. 234.
14. Ibid., Loc. 498.
15. Ibid.
16. Ibid., Loc. 552.
17. Ibid.
18. Ibid., Loc. 794.
19. Ibid., Loc. 1049.
20. Ibid.

CHAPTER THREE

Going Out to Them

"Shortly before dawn Jesus
went out to them, walking
on the lake."

MATTHEW 14:25

One of the major challenges black congregations are facing in engaging this new generation of would-be disciples actually stems from an essential part of the historic ethos of the black church. Throughout the history of the black church in the U.S., the church's physical building often provided sanctuary and safe space for spiritual development, community engagement, strategic planning, and civil disobedience. When public education was widely unavailable (or illegal) in many states across the Union, it was inside the church buildings where Sunday school classes doubled as literacy clinics for poor black pupils from week to week. Throughout the Civil Rights movement in America, black churches opened the doors of their edifices to house rallies and strategic planning meetings to push various causes forward.

Speak to black Baby Boomers who "grew up" in church and they no doubt have treasure chests of stories about the hours they spent going to the "church house" during the week. On Sundays, they were present for Sunday school, morning worship, afternoon worship services at "sister churches," and BTU (Baptist Training Union) in the evening. During the week, there were mandatory trips to choir rehearsals, drill team practices, Bible studies, and prayer meetings. Outside of specific congregational programs, many black churches created schools, drama clubs, sporting leagues, and fine arts programs—all designed to encourage congregants and members of the community to come to the church building and participate in the life of the church throughout the week. One of the recurring mottos you will hear in many African American congregations tells how generations of churchgoers have viewed the role of the church's location in the process of Christian development: "Everything we need is in the house!"

The turn of the twenty-first century has left many congregations scratching their heads about how to get this generation of young people to come into the doors of our churches and to participate in the ministries we offer. This challenge is not confined to smaller congregations with fewer bells and whistles than their megachurch counterparts. In the congregation where I serve in Houston, Texas, we engage thousands of young people every Sunday morning for worship, a trend many of our young adults have attributed to the preaching of our pastor and the music ministry of the church. However, the vast majority of these same disciples simply will not come to the church throughout the week to participate in the ministry opportunities we offer "in the house."

This is where I think the story of Jesus walking on the lake is incredibly helpful to consider. Continuing with the metaphor of Jesus as the Christian church and Peter and the disciples in the boat as the Millennials we seek to engage, Jesus' approach to engaging the disciples in Matthew 14 is instructive. After spending some time alone to pray, Jesus had a few options. It was late, so he could easily have come down the mountain and slept for the rest of the evening, choosing to wait until morning either for the disciples to come back from the other side of the lake or for him to hitch a ride to meet them on the other side. Alternatively, given Jesus' water-walking abilities, he could have chosen to speed-walk across the lake to Gennesaret and waited for the disciples to come to him on the shore. In the end, Jesus makes a simple yet profound decision in verse 25: *he goes out to them.*

The Winds of Change

While the biblical text is not explicit about Jesus' motivation for going out to the disciples in the boat, we can imagine that his motivation has something to do with the environment that the disciples are in by verse 25. When the disciples originally departed from Jesus in verse 22, there was no mention of a storm, violent winds, or rough surf. Yet by the time Jesus concluded his solitary time on the mountainside, the winds that would have helped to produce an initial push for the disciples to sail away have changed. The waves have seemingly picked up and the winds are now against the boat, placing the disciples under very different conditions than those they had sailed through in previous verses. Without doubt, it is Jesus' sensitivity to the change in climate and the subsequent effects on the disciples that prompts him to be proactive. He cannot wait for the disciples to somehow get to him. He knows he must go out to them.

At this point I need to stop and make an important announcement: the winds have changed! Many of our pastors and leadership teams are frustrated today by the inability to "get these young people to *come out*" to various ministry opportunities, Bible studies, and special events—in large part because they have not given much consideration to the fact that the winds have changed in the way that young people engage the material and content they want and need. In the end, a lot of church resources and staff hours are wasted putting on "Millennial" versions of Bible studies, worship services, and programs, waiting for young disciples to show up on to the shores of our sanctuaries who will likely never come (certainly not beyond Sunday morning worship). This observation is not to suggest that we end our weekly Bible study offerings, worship services, or ministry programming; often the issue for this generation is not a disinterest in the *material* that the church has to provide, but a disconnect in the *method* of delivery.

Think about it: black Millennials belong to a generation referred to as digital natives. They have grown up daily utilizing the kind of technological advances that for previous generations was only the stuff of science fiction! In 2016, the most utilized tool for black Millennials was the smartphone, and most young adults are programmed to have access to just about anything they want, anywhere they want, at any time they want (well, as long as their phone retains a decent charge).

Many Millennials are taking advantage of the increasingly lucrative opportunities to work remotely for their employers, participating in everything from staff business meetings to television interviews from the comfort of their kitchens, bedrooms, or home offices. Direct-to-consumer service providers such as FreshDirect and Instacart allow Millennials to order their weekly groceries from anywhere and have them delivered to their doors for a nominal delivery fee. With the explosion of streaming television services (Netflix, Hulu, Amazon Video) and on-demand content provided by many television networks, this generation no longer has to wait an entire week to watch the next episode of their favorite shows. They can "binge watch" entire seasons of the latest television sensation in one sitting. In short, the new norm for this generation's content consumption is clear: everything from shopping and business meetings to video-streamed conversations with family and friends can be experienced through a smart device at any time that works for them, from anywhere that works for them.

Well, everything except New Members' Orientation classes at their local church. While churches bemoan the absence of these young adults from their standard six- or twelve-week discipleship training courses, many inquisitive black Millennials have already obtained the needed information through their favorite YouTube personality. What, then, shall we say to these issues? How can churches better engage this generation of young people whose technological wiring has made unlimited and unrestrictive access to the content they desire and need normative? As is normally the case, the church's best bet is to follow Jesus. We have to go out to them—to the people we want to reach.

New Platforms Versus New Programming

One of the great blessings of congregants knowing you are work-ing on a doctorate is that they want to engage you in conver-sation *anytime* they see or hear anything remotely connected to the topic they've heard you are studying. Such was the case as I completed my doctoral research at Virginia Union University. On one particular Sunday morning, one of our members chased me down between services to get my opinion on a flyer he saw on Facebook. What was being advertised was the unveiling of a brand-new "Millennial Worship Experience" at one of our sister churches, and the member wanted to know my opinion about the new service. "Aren't you researching those *Millenniums*, Rev.?" the member asked me sincerely. "Don't you think we need to do something like that here?"

It took me a moment to answer his question because I didn't want to make an unfair assessment based on limited information (and because what I really was trying to do before the member stopped me was get to the restroom before the start of the next service). I applauded and appreciated our sister church's awareness that this demographic and generation has unique characteristics that require the church to engage them differently. The flyer made it clear that the service would only last one hour—perfect for a generation that communicates in 140-character statements and 10-second video intervals. However, the rest of the flyer seemed to communicate only a flashier, hipper version of the worship service that the church already held, with a few more lights, a more popular worship leader, and louder music. The goal was obvious: changing the face and sound of the congregation's normal worship service in an attempt to attract more young people to the church. After a few seconds of pulling my thoughts together and swaying from side to side (I had to go!), I provided the member with a short but honest response: "The answer is not more *attraction*; the answer is more *access*."

Our study helped illuminate a simple yet powerful truth about black Millennials and their relationship with church programming.

More than 80 percent of black Millennials who show up in our churches at least once a month believe that discipleship and teaching ministry offerings of our churches like Sunday school and mid-week Bible studies are essential to their spiritual development, yet only one-third of these same young people actually take advantage of such programming.

Where is the disconnect? The answer lies in *when* the material is offered, which is even more important than who is providing the material. (We will explore this dynamic in later chapters.) While the personality and style of the teacher is a major factor in why black Millennials do not participate in ministry programming, the day of the week and time of day that programming is offered are the top two reasons these young people are not consistently participating in the discipleship development programming offered by their churches during the week. In many cases, the content these young people desire is simply not available at a time when they are available to access it. With this in mind, the challenge of the church is not necessarily to create more programming that young adults may or may not be able to attend, but to build new platforms that offer the same content in formats that can be accessed in a way that is normal for a generation of digital natives—anytime and anywhere.

One of the greatest joys I have as Minister to Youth and College Students in my church is leading our weekly college ministry Bible study experience called "The Brook." Each week students from the surrounding college campuses come to the church for a hot meal and the opportunity to engage the Bible in a forum that allows for discussion and discovery amongst a community of other young believers.

February is always the month where we have the largest attendance at The Brook because of the popularity of our annual "Sex, Snapchat, and the Scriptures" series. The series seeks to answer the question, "How can a young person keep his or her ways pure in our digitally connected and overly sexualized culture?" Students pack the fellowship hall of our church to ask questions concerning issues around human sexuality and the Scriptures.

Nothing is off limits in our discussion—from the spiritual and relational implications of "sexting" our boyfriends or girlfriends (or random attractive strangers) to conversations about the Christian disciple's use of vibrators, sex toys, and Internet pornography. As the facilitator, I am always encouraged in February when I stand in the back of the room and look at all of the students who have chosen to attend. *"They're here!"* I often think to myself. *"Finally, we have cracked the code to get them here!"*

You can imagine my hurt, then, when a student burst my prideful bubble one night following a session on masturbation and pornography. The student approached me and said, "Rev., thank you so much for the lesson. You confirmed a lot of what Joe Solomon has been teaching!" Before I could ask her who Joe was, she pulled up a YouTube video starring Bro. Joe, a young Christian poet who produces a weekly series of video "webisodes" where he teaches on various hot-button topics. As I watched the short video, no more than ten minutes in length, I had to concur with the student. Many of the main ideas from my lesson were echoed in Joe's video. The major difference was obvious. While 50 students came to hear me teach this (awesome) lesson in one sitting, being offered one time a year, Joe's similar, shorter lesson had been viewed more than 70,000 times!

I walked away from that exchange with an invaluable insight that will aid churches seeking to engage black Millennials more effectively: *focus on creating new platforms to host your most important content.* As illustrated in my encounter with the student, these young people are hungry for the Word of God and for godly instruction in important areas of their lives. But many are gleaning this instruction from platform offerings outside the church. While most churches are focusing on creating new programming to attract Millennials to our buildings, it may be more important to supply the content these young people are yearning for on platforms that can be accessed more naturally to them.

To be sure, this is not an either-or proposition. I am not advocating destroying your midweek Bible study in the church conference room or fellowship hall. But what might it look like to follow up that real-time experience by recording a five-minute recap video of the main points of your lesson to be posted on the church website, Facebook page, or YouTube channel? Instantly, this valuable content that is craved by the masses is not solely experienced by the 50 congregants who can make it to the church that evening, but it can be viewed, reviewed, shared, and digested anytime and anywhere. This is the Millennial way, and churches will do well by acknowledging and adjusting to it!

Where Do We Start? Expanding Your Digital Landscape

The Website

Does anyone remember the Yellow Pages? As a child I would search the Yellow Pages, that huge book of phone numbers, addresses, and brief descriptions of the businesses operating near me. These days those bulky yellow books have become obsolete, replaced by Internet search engines such as Google or crowd-sourcing sites such as Yelp. Millennials (and just about everyone else) will turn to the web to get information about the companies, organizations, and services that they seek with regularity, and a company's website is often a primary factor in whether a young person will invest time and talent in that organization's products or services. To be sure, as this trend is true for the dining, shopping, and business experiences of black Millennials, the web presence of a church is also a key determinant for these young adults seeking to find an appropriate faith community to fellowship and with which to grow.

Let me be clear: in the twenty-first century, a church's online presence is a must! Moreover, a congregation should not have a church website simply to be able to say they have a website. To serve this present age, churches must *invest* in the maintenance of their online platforms with the same seriousness as they invest in the maintenance of their brick and mortar structures. This begins with the creation (or updating) of a beautiful church website and homepage.

Some would-be young disciples may hear about your congregation and drive by the church building to check out a service or Bible study, but many more will hear about the congregation and make an initial "drive-by" of the church's website. This is why the look, feel, imagery, and design of a church website are as essential as the architecture and landscaping of the church's facilities. Black Millennials will make determinations about the type of congregation a church is long before they ever step into the building, based on the optics and design they encounter on the website. As technology continues to evolve and website design trends change for the other sectors of society, churches should be intentional about updating and refreshing the design of their website to provide an experience that is consistent with other online platforms black Millennials frequently engage. Vibrant, clear, colorful images and videos that feature the worship experiences, community service and activism efforts, children and young people, and the pastoral leadership all help to communicate volumes to would-be disciples about the ethos of a church community.

Let me pause here to provide some important clarification. Throughout this book, I will acknowledge the importance of the personality of the congregation's leader in black Millennials' willingness to engage with a particular ministry. For better or worse, the pastor or public leader of the congregation *is* central to the worship experience and spiritual formation process of the congregation, and that prominence should be reflected in the online presence of the church. *However,* overindulgence in this principle can be disastrous for congregations. Full-page banners of the senior pastor in the classic model pose beside a miniature picture of the congregation or church building may communicate more to black Millennials than the church intends. While it is important for them to be able to easily identify who the leader is, modest and balanced imagery is important to prevent congregations from communicating that the *pastor* is the focus in that ministry context. While the pastor is important to black Millennials, it is more important that they are in a faith community that will lead them to a genuine and powerful encounter with God.

Social Media

Our study indicates that the number one place for black Millennials to get their news and be informed of important events is through social media, which has effectively dethroned television, radio, and newspaper outlets for this generation. In many ways, this reality provides a great opportunity for churches seeking to attract, engage, and develop Millennial disciples of Christ. Gone are the days when ministries needed to pay a lot of money to engage the next generation through television or radio ministries. While these ministries are still effective for a segment of the population, an Internet connection and mobile device are all that are needed for churches of the twenty-first century to get valuable content into the hands of new generations.

At the time of this writing, Facebook and YouTube are the most far-reaching social media outlets, and churches would do well to ensure that announcements, sermons, and other Christian educational content are made available through these media. YouTube now has the capability for organizations and users to upload long-form video for free, and congregations who simply want to expand their digital footprints should consider placing quality sermons and Bible studies on the site. What may be lost in bookstore or media ministry sales by uploading content to a free, video-sharing website may be gained many times over through the wide-reaching access to people that these sites provide.

As we discuss building new platforms via social media, I must provide a few important words of caution. First, the platform you utilize should match the audience you seek to reach. For example, when Facebook was originally created, only users who had a college or university email could access it. The exclusiveness of the platform made it the social place to be—until Facebook expanded to include anyone with an email address. As too many grandparents, pokes, and game requests began to overpopulate the Facebook world, Millennials began to migrate away from Facebook as their primary social media "hangout." Quicker, less complex platforms such as Twitter, Instagram, and Snapchat became the preferred social media platforms.

This is important for churches to consider because, while I would advise a church to continue with its Facebook page, the primary audience on this platform will likely not be the Millennials, but their parents who came and made it "uncool." I encourage congregations to invite Millennial members who are responsible and frequent users of social media to work on the church's social media efforts. They know the technology, but they can also shed light on where the new digital hangouts are. It is important for congregations to stay connected and informed as new applications and digital spaces are created each day, and to recognize that what may be a viable social media platform today may be obsolete in a few weeks or months. For this reason, I advise churches to fall in love with the process of quality content creation and not the platform itself. *Where* we post and provide our content will change as the technology changes, but the content itself can be perfected.

To Stream or Not to Stream? That Is the Question

I recently had the privilege of preaching at a church that does an incredible job of attracting black Millennials. The music was incredible, the worship was spirited and genuine, and the people were loving and compassionate. After preaching the first service, I asked the pastor how I could share the live stream (or live broadcast via the internet) of the next service with my wife. His answer surprised me. "We don't stream," he said. "Our content isn't yet strong enough to warrant the investment." I pondered that thought, and while at first I was shocked to hear the admission, I later appreciated his honesty and humility to make such an evaluation of the congregation he was serving. He understood that to stream is literally to open a congregation up to the world, and it is important to think through whether or not we are prepared to present ourselves on a worldwide stage.

In the same way that the quality and imagery of a church's website communicate something about the kind of church people can expect to attend, the quality and definition of the images presented in a church's stream speak to the quality of the worship experience that visitors can expect to participate in. Grainy and distorted video can be a major turnoff for black Millennials, especially in an age where professional artists are creating high-definition, broadcast-quality video content from their iPhones.

As local congregations deliberate whether or not to stream worship experiences, they must also ask what they are willing to invest in these experiences. While free social media streaming options such as Facebook Live are available, they may be better suited for short, personal broadcasts than as the primary streaming medium for a congregation. Consider the strength of your sermonic and worship and arts presentations, and investigate how much your congregation is willing to invest. Then decide on an effective strategy to provide the best-quality stream possible, if your congregation is ready for the exposure (and scrutiny) of the worldwide stage.

Mobile Giving

In 2016, *USA Today* reported that Millennials make more than 50 percent of their shopping purchases online.[1] Online financial transactions are normative for black Millennials (many never carry cash or checks), and churches invested in the spiritual formation of this generation must take this reality into consideration as we build our online presence. Online giving options are essential tools for congregations as they provide opportunities for digital natives to invest financially in the life of the church at anytime, anywhere in the world, and in a way they are accustomed to spending their money. Some churches choose not to offer online giving because of the costs associated with processing the online transactions, but the benefits outweigh the minimal costs. Online giving platforms such as Givelify and SecureGive are good starting places for churches beginning their search for affordable online giving platforms.

Not all online giving platforms are the same, nor will all online giving platforms satisfy the user preferences of black Millennials. It is important to note that digital natives desire a user platform that is easy to navigate. If there are too many steps involved in the process of giving, churches run the risk of losing the financial interest of the Millennials who seek to invest in them. Seek online giving platforms that provide a one-time setup for users, where congregants can provide their credit or debit card and billing information one time and then quickly sign in to their accounts to give future gifts. Options to direct-deposit tithes and offerings from bank accounts are also helpful to young adults seeking to automate their financial responsibilities. Ultimately, these investments will only increase the willingness of black Millennials to engage in the totality of the life of the church and her work.

Breaking Out of the Box: New Physical Spaces

"Going out to them" also means rethinking where sacred space can be made. It is almost cliché to hear people talk about going "beyond the walls of the church house" to do ministry, but this is a must in ministry to and with Millennials. As stated in Chapter Two, the main impediment to black Millennial engagement in the church is not a disinterest in the content, but limitations in accessing that content. With this in mind, it may be helpful for churches to consider spaces outside of the church campus for engaging in spiritual formation.

In my study, black Millennials were asked, "In what spaces outside of the church building (cyberspaces included) would you want to engage in the teaching ministries of the church?" The most popular space was in online communities such as online videos, online classes, and online chats. The second most popular response was also online through social media outlets, including Twitter, Facebook Live, Periscope, YouTube, and Snapchat. However, the third most popular response was holding teaching ministry opportunities in home or small-group settings. Respondents also suggested holding teaching ministry experiences at local coffee houses, restaurants or lounges, and other community spaces. With a bit of creativity and feedback from the Millennials in the congregation, local churches can find new places in which to engage in spiritual formation that are inviting for this generation of young adults.

Consistency and Overcoming Challenges

As churches seek to build new platforms of engagement, they may not see the initial results they hope to see. It is important to remember that the first key to establishing effective platforms is consistency. Consistency is critical to building traction and tribes, so whatever schedule is set for the distribution of content, be faithful to it.

Second, as previously stated, fall in love with the process of creating great content, not with the platform itself. The content we create must be captivating and relatable and hit on the core issues that are important to Millennials. (We will discuss this further in later chapters.)

Third, to make these platforms work at an optimal level, churches should be prepared for some associated costs and expect to make an initial financial investment. As technology continues to improve, however, congregations will be able to do a lot more with less.

Finally, if you are a pastor or church leader who has read all of this and you are still clueless on how to move forward, consider bringing on a young staffer or intern to help manage your platforms and produce the content. In the end, God's kingdom will benefit and possibilities will be sparked by the willingness of the church to come toward the "Peters" in our midst!

VALUABLE VOICES

Featured Millennial: Joseph A. C. Smith, age 33, President of Joseph A. C. Smith Ministries, Inc., Former Assistant to the Pastor at Alfred Street Baptist Church, Alexandria, VA

On effective models of ministry to black Millennials within traditional church settings . . .

One of the things that seems to be working in traditional settings is the promulgation of a more relevant gospel message. Millennials are deeply interested in things that directly affect our daily lives. We tend to be a lot less interested in theoretical messages and much more interested in praxis. In recent years, it seems that there's been an uptick in younger pastors taking the helm of traditional churches, and these pastors, in many instances, bring with them an approach to gospel teaching and preaching that seeks to directly improve the listener's day-to-day activities and relationships. Millennials love this kind of teaching, and if the current trend holds, churches who employ this kind of gospel teaching will continue to attract Millennials by the droves.

Online streaming and e-churches are also increasingly popular with Millennials. Convenience is so extremely important in our culture, and traditional churches are beginning to adopt tools and technology that make it easier for people to encounter God and engage in the work of the church. Mission-minded churches have for decades highlighted the importance of "getting out of the four walls and taking the church to the people who need it," and this concept has taken new meaning in the Digital Age, especially as mobile phones eclipse computers as the leading source for information, communication, and entertainment. Churches who don't offer online streaming are probably not growing with the Millennial population.

One of the things I was blessed to do while at Alfred Street was to start a social media ministry to provide visibility for the church in the social media space. Not only was it an incredible way to engage Millennials in ministry work, surprisingly, it gave all the visual artists in our church—the graphic designers, photographers, videographers, cartoonist, etc.—a place to use their gifts as well. From the very beginning, we had 20 or 30 people who showed up with so many incredible ideas.

I initially created a framework organized around the different media platforms (Facebook, Twitter, Instagram), but that model didn't effectively support all the visual artists who were showing up to use their gifts. With God's help, we created a new framework built around two major prongs: content and distribution. Most of the team leads and members were Millennials.

On creating his own digital platforms . . .

For me, Christ was incredibly relevant and fresh in his approach to ministry. People could relate to the stories he told and his methods were cutting-edge and state-of-the-art. His message was sound and compelling and was shared in a way that made people take notice. I am simply following the model Christ left us.

Churches are often the first to resist and the last to adopt emerging technologies, which is antithetical to any idea or effort of being relevant. I have tried to be an early adopter of new technologies as a means of sharing the gospel message, and so far it seems to be having an incredible impact. When a new digital platform emerges, I study it and try to learn everything I can about it and how to engage people using it. When Periscope launched, I was goofing off one morning on my ride to work, jamming to Anthony Brown and Group Therapy. About 20 or 30 people found the broadcast, and by the end of the broadcast people were saying, "We'll see you tomorrow, same time, same place."

I found myself logging on the next morning and many mornings after that, and more and more people kept tuning in. God has grown that platform to over 20,000 followers and The Morning Hype now averages anywhere from 450 to 1,000 viewers whenever we are on. Learning the platform and how to use it to engage audiences was key. God provided the wind, but I had to learn how to raise the sail. Everything from selecting the right title for the broadcasts, to lighting, to even my voice tone and cadence had to be considered. All of it matters for effective communication, especially when sharing something as important and essential as the gospel.

First steps for churches looking to build digital spaces and platforms . . .

Without a doubt, the very first thing a church should do is find a team of Millennials and other youth to lead the effort. They know the technologies and how to use them. Generally speaking, if a Millennial attends your church regularly, he or she believes in the mission and work of your church—otherwise they probably wouldn't attend. Very often, church-going Millennials are seeking community and a place to belong and be accepted. Inviting them to use their gift to add value to your ministry is precisely the kind of affirmation and acceptance that leads to long-term commitments and constituency.

Suggestions for congregations seeking to attract and engage in the spiritual formation process of black Millennials . . .

Sunday school and Bible study are antiquated tools that are not very effective in reaching Millennials. Christian education is critically important but declining rapidly, and this is due mainly to the poor efforts of churches to modernize their approach and offerings in this area. Churches should strongly consider digital options for Christian education. Things like e-classrooms, webinars, etc., are great tools to begin incorporating as key elements of our ministry.

Remember, the goal is no longer to get as many people as possible to attend your brick and mortar church; the goal is to impact as many people as we can, as often as we can, with the gospel of Jesus Christ. The energy and effort it takes to prepare a Sunday school lesson for 10 regular in-person attendees could also be used to establish a digital Sunday school classroom that engages 100 unique users on a daily basis. What once reached only 10 people now touches 500 to 700 people per week, when optimized.

In Mark 2, Jesus reminds us, in his statement about new wine and old wineskins, about the critical importance of the elasticity of mind and method. What a fatality it will be for the church if we continue to put our wine in cracked bottles.

Walking on Water

1. What are your congregation's current evangelistic efforts? How effective have they been in drawing black Millennials?

2. As a team, assess your digital landscaping. How is your church website? What is your current social media presence? Does your church accommodate online giving? What are areas of improvement?

3. Can you identify any "hot spots" in the community where young adults frequent? Imagine a ministry offering in these places. What would it look like?

Notes

1. Eli Blumenthal, "Millennials drive spike in online shopping," *USA Today*, June 8, 2016, accessed April 1, 2017, http://www.usatoday.com/story/money/2016/06/08/survey-more-than-half-purchases-made-online/85592598/.

"It's a Ghost"

When the disciples saw
him walking on the lake,
they were terrified. "It's
a ghost," they said, and
cried out in fear. But Jesus
immediately said to them:
"Take courage! It is I.
Don't be afraid."

MATTHEW 14:26-27

When we pick up on the Matthew 14 saga in verse 26, we find Jesus making the important decision to "go to them," but not without conflict or confusion. As Jesus journeys toward his disciples in the boat, presumably to help them through the storm and to journey with them toward their ultimate destination, the disciples see him from the boat and are terrified! To be fair to the disciples, they had just spent the entire day with Jesus doing ministry and the entire night sailing in hopes of safely getting to "the other side." It's possible that their tired eyes could have just been playing tricks on them. But after collectively wiping the crust from their eyes and readjusting their gaze, the human-shaped figure is still there. Walking toward them. On the lake.

OMG! For most of the disciples in the boat, the only intelligible thing they can blurt out is, "It's a ghost!" and the shock of what they are seeing and experiencing silences them for the remainder of the ordeal. Yet there is one among them who, after hearing this "ghost" respond to their cry, is willing to engage with the figure before them. In this scene, both the speech of Peter and the silence of his fellow disciples in the boat are telling and helpful in our conversation around reengaging and making disciples of this unique generation in our churches.

Scared into Silence

For many of the disciples in the boat, the sight of a "ghost"—an organism that appears to be alive but is actually not—is enough to scare them into silence. After all, interacting with ghosts was probably not covered in their fishermen handbooks or training sessions. Moreover, the disciples have legitimate reasons to fear this perceived ghost on the lake.

One of the greatest challenges for the individuals in this scene is the considerable distance between the disciples in the boat and the "ghost" on the lake. There is enough distance that the disciples are unable to clearly make out *what* and *whom* they are preparing to encounter. What they do perceive—a figure walking on the lake—is not a possible feat for typical human beings, and if this figure could walk on water, what else could it do?

Moreover, this "ghost" is coming *toward* them! I imagine that, prior to Matthew 14, some of them had exchanged ghost stories on their many nights fishing on the Sea of Galilee—stories that likely painted ghosts as evil spirits from the other world sent to torment the living with their supernatural power. *What could this ghost want with them? What was this ghost's agenda? Could this ghost inflict the same kind of harm and pain that they heard about in the stories?* In the end, conversing with the ghost is not an option for most of the disciples in the boat; the best they can do is cry out in fear.

Unfortunately, a lot of Millennials share some of these same fears and concerns as they view our churches. While there are some young adults who are disengaged from the church due to a lack of interest in the programming or the personality of the preacher, this Scripture text points us to a set of young people who are in a different boat. For these young people, their lack of engagement is not birthed out of a lack of interest, but out of their fear of a seemingly "dead" organism. Without doubt, some of the same questions running through the minds of the disciples in Matthew 14 are the same questions running through the minds of young adults today viewing the church's presence in the twenty-first century: *What is the church's agenda? What does the church want with me? If I try engaging this ghost, could it inflict the same kind of harm and pain that I've heard stories about?*

What Is the Church's Agenda?

The question of the Christian church's agenda in the twenty-first century is an unavoidable one for congregations seeking to engage black Millennials. Transparency is key! As digital natives who are educated and influenced primarily through the use of images, sound bites, and video content, many of these young people's views of the church, her pastors, and her agenda are shaped by mass media long before they ever enter our church buildings. In most cases, this is not a good thing for the church.

The latest pastoral sex scandals are shared with the entire world within minutes through the social media platforms that black Millennials cannot seem to live without. Cable news networks cement stories in our minds of pedophilia and abuse in the pews through 24-hour news cycle loops. From famous musicians parodying ignorant preachers to reality television spots that highlight the vehicles and mansions of some of the most popular names in the gospel ministry, black Millennials have been fed a narrative of the church and its leaders as ignorant, insincere, hypocritical, money-hungry, and often behind-the-times.

While these depictions and caricatures of the church and pastoral leadership are not new, in the age of social media these images are more prominent and widely spread than ever. The result is a generation that does not trust the church with the same ease its predecessors did. In many cases, it is a generation suspicious of the church's agenda and why it is seeking them to come into the fold.

What Does the Church Want with Me?

Black Millennials' distrust concerning the agenda of twenty-first century churches makes it imperative that congregations be as transparent as possible about their internal operations and become masters in the art of "telling their story." These young people want to know why the ghost is approaching them. *Are you seeking to love me to life and direct me toward a transformative relationship with Jesus Christ and community, or am I simply another number to add to your church's roll who you hope will also help keep your church from slipping into foreclosure?*

Even if the honest answer is some combination of the two, which would be fine if it were communicated in the right way, congregational transparency is key! If tithes and offerings are being used to keep the lights on and support the hardworking staff of the church, don't be afraid to make that clear. In giving campaigns and weekly offering appeals, make it clear that the tithes and offerings are not being given to finance the senior pastor's new private jet (unless they are, in which case that needs to be clearly stated). Demonstrate that building fund contributions are being used to build something!

It should come as no surprise that a number of young adults have zero interest in financially supporting important projects of their church because of distrust developed by contribution patterns in other congregational experiences. By contrast, a significant number of young adults would be more than willing to engage and support the work of the church if they knew more about what their congregations were involved in.

For this reason, "telling the story" is key, chronicling the work and ministry of the church through videos, photographs, and sound bites and providing prominent venues for these stories to be told to the congregation and community. When the great work, vision, and ministry of our churches is displayed and disclosed in responsible ways—through video recaps, newsletter photo montages, social media posts, etc.—it endears black Millennials to the work and vision of the congregation and increases their willingness to engage.

If I Engage This Ghost, Will It Inflict Harm and Pain on Me, Too?

While working on my doctoral research, I spent a lot of time following church-oriented conversations of black Millennials on social media platforms. While I chose not to use these tweets and Facebook threads in the research, these conversations helped shed tremendous light on the stories of black Millennials in various points of engagement with the church.

Most interesting for me were conversations primarily led by black Millennials who identified as both Christian and members of the LGBTQ community. Clear patterns emerged from these conversations. While many still professed an unwavering love for God, they were no longer willing to engage in community with the Church. The reasons almost always tied back to personal or familial stories of hurt experienced at the hands of the body of Christ. In many cases, this hurt had taken years to recover from. In the end, the risk of being injured by the church was too great, and rather than conversing with the ghost on the water, many elected to wait for Jesus on other shores. In short, they feared the ghost would hurt them.

"Church hurt" and the threat of future hurt is a major deterrent to Millennial engagement in our congregations. Again, "church hurt" is by no means a new phenomenon, but the prevalence of digital technology causes these stories to spread wider and faster. Congregations who are serious about engaging these young adults must be honest about the secret abuses, traditions, and not-so-secret "-isms" (sexism, classism, ageism, etc.) that exist within our congregations and that have inflicted harm on our parishioners.

To be clear, this is not a call for the church to slip into a state of spiritual relativity or to lower God's standard in an attempt to please everyone who walks in our doors. On the contrary, the church must revere God's Word and God's people enough to seek faithfully to mine truth and to divorce it from the human traditions that unduly harm those who come to the sanctuary in search of what "thus saith the Lord."

"My Sheep Know My Voice"

As the disciples were crying out in fear from the boat, Jesus continued to walk toward them. As he heard their cries and desired to calm their fears, he had to decide the best way to engage them. He could keep walking toward them, maybe even faster than before, but doing so might only frighten them more. Approaching them too fast could cause them to try to steer the boat in the opposite direction and sail away before he could get close enough for them to see who he truly was. Considering the power of the wind and the waves that were against them, an attempt by the disciples to steer away from Jesus might have turned out disastrous for them and put them in a more dangerous situation. In the end, Jesus took a different course of action. He remained where he was and spoke to them. "Take courage! It is I. Don't be afraid."

The amazing piece of this section of the story is that Peter can correctly identify the "I" who is speaking to him! Given the distance between Jesus and the disciples, and the waves that contributed to the disciples' increased anxiety and decreased visibility, the "I" speaking to them could have been *anybody*. The safer bet may have been for Jesus to say more specifically, "Take courage! It is I, Jesus! Don't be afraid." Yet even without Jesus clearly identifying himself by name, Peter was able to assess that the "I" was Jesus—presumably because he could recognize his friend and teacher's beloved voice. Again, the ability to recognize even a familiar voice would be no easy feat considering all of the circumstances surrounding the saga on the lake, but Peter's immediate *recognition* of Jesus was grounded in an extended *relationship* developed with Jesus.

Relationship-building is an essential task for any congregation seeking to engage black Millennials in the work and ministry of the church. To be sure, the task of relationship-building extends far beyond church leadership knowing the names and faces of individual congregants on Sunday morning (although this is a helpful tactic). Effective relationship-building here requires congregations to build the infrastructure to maintain awareness of the significant moments and movements in the lives of its individual congregants, while also becoming a persistent presence in the everyday lives of the young adults it seeks to serve.

This is likely a challenge for many churches, especially those that have become "commuter congregations" where the bulk of the membership no longer lives in the community where the church building is located. Yet, it is a challenge worth strategizing to solve. Individually, this could mean empowering and equipping church leaders to help responsibly shepherd small groups of the congregation (often based on age demographics or shared community) through "check-ins," fellowships, or Bible study sessions. Corporately, the key is not stringing together a few "pop-up" community events that are great for photo-ops and news clippings, but rather narrowing down necessary and continual investments in the community.

How might our communities and congregations change if we invested in providing tutorials, childcare services (do you know how much childcare costs are these days?), and after-school programming for young parents in the community? What if our church sanctuary and classroom spaces doubled as space to teach English and Spanish to brothers and sisters in an increasingly bilingual society? Relationship-building benefits us all, and where there is a sense of *relationship* established, young disciples such as Peter feel safe enough to *respond*.

VALUABLE VOICES

Featured Millennial: Kay Williams, age 35, Education Management Specialist, Houston, TX

I joined the church when I was about 23 years old and initially I got very involved in their middle and high school ministries. I have a degree in curriculum and instruction and I'm a certified teacher so I started volunteering with their after-school programs and even wrote grants and helped the church secure money for their programs. I wasn't a staff member, I was still volunteering. I didn't realize how sometimes in churches, when people see a gift that someone has, instead of receiving the gift and nurturing the gift and loving on that person, they sometimes use it for their benefit. Eventually, because I was volunteering so much with the church and I started writing grants for their programs I was approached by the senior pastor and one of the minister's wives at the church (who will be referred to as "Cindy" throughout the remainder of the interview) with an opportunity to come on staff as they were launching a nonprofit portion of the church. I thought, this is my church—they love me and I love them. Why not? So I went in blindly; I didn't even really know about a salary. I just knew, "Hey, you are going to be able to really work in the church." I ended up putting in two weeks notice at the job I was working for at the time and left my job as a site director and program director to go be the executive director of this nonprofit arm of the church. That's the position I was *told* I would have.

Things were good that first year. It's similar to a marriage or in a relationship. It's like the honeymoon phase. Not only was I doing what I was employed to do but I also started to get more involved in ministry at the church—I sang in the choir, l led the Theater Arts Ministry, taught youth Bible study, led youth conferences, recruited volunteers—just passionate and excited to serve in my church. But after that first year, things got sticky. They got sticky because the minister's wife who had recruited me, Cindy, began to use her age and her level of influence to basically bully me. If there was anything that I disagreed with at a committee meeting, she would run and go tell the pastor. That bullying began to boil over and affect my health. I suffer from migraines sometimes and they began to flare up more frequently—but I kept saying to myself, "God has me here for a reason and when he wants to move me, he will move me," because I had experienced ill-treatment at the job I had before coming to the church. I guess I felt the church was going to save me from the ill treatment I experienced at the last job. I was young and naïve, working and serving because that's the right thing to do—not seeing that I was being used.

Everything came to a head while I was working as the program director for our summer program. Part of my responsibilities were buying meals and breakfast items and snacks for children who are there. One of my workers said, "Hey, we don't have any more cereal. We don't have any breakfast items." [It was too late to get a check request processed] so I had to go to Sam's Club to buy some stuff in bulk and I used the company card. When I brought the receipt in and [the woman who was always giving me hell] found out I used the card to benefit something for the program, she called the pastor on me. I was called into the office about it. He said, "Sister girl, you need to respect your elders. Don't you know why we hired you?" I realized that I was basically a pawn.

I went to my doctor because it started to really weigh itself on me. My doctor told me, she said, "You're sick. You are sick. You're having too many migraines. I'm questionable on the medication I'm giving you. Your back is hurting you. I'm prescribing you three days off. You have to take the days off. You cannot continue to go to work." I took my letter to my supervisors and the pastor and everything at the church and said, "I need to take leave." The response was,

"Oh, we're a church. You know we don't work on leave.
People just do what they want to do, except for you, Sister
girl, you need to be there."

When I reiterated that my doctor ordered the three days
off the response was, "Well, since you have to take off, we're
just going to let you go because what you have going on is
going to cause an issue here." Being let go and being told I
would be let go, I'm thinking, "I only have two weeks left in
this program. Please let me stay." Literally begging for my job
and neglecting my health wanting to help the church because
the church is supposed to love me. The church is supposed
to be there to support me. I came back to work the next day
and my manager told me I had to go, waited for me to pack
everything into a box, walked me out like I was thief, like I
was some kind of criminal, and asked that the security guard
for the church make sure that I never come on the property
again, all because I asked for three days off.

I think back on the person I was then, because when
they let me go, what was also painful was that I had no
other option set up, no back-up plans because I thought
the church would never do me that way. I was ineligible
for unemployment. Others were eligible. I found out after
contacting Workforce Commission that they purposely said,
"No, she cannot get unemployment benefits." It was like
they were intentionally trying to get back at me. I'm able
to talk about it now without crying because I cried literally
for three and a half months, every time I pulled up to the
church. [I stayed as a member for a time even after I was
laid off.]

On the role of leadership in "church hurt." . . .

Some churches use people. And it often begins with poor
leadership choices. Just because a person says they're willing
to [effectively lead] doesn't mean they're able. In my case,
the people that the [pastoral leadership] put in leadership

to recruit [a person like me] who had a fire for God and for church—[those leaders] trounced on that and used me in a way that caused my progress to be halted for five years. Some lead with the wrong motives, doing things because they want a title and not because they care. So, when people who do care come and work, [those leaders] are mad because it appears that others are trying to outshine them. I saw that in my own situation. *God* gave me that skill. *God* gave me that drive. *God* gave me the ability to connect with these people. Just because he didn't give *you* that doesn't mean you have to kill me, doesn't mean you got to take me out, doesn't mean you have to conspire, you have to burn my name, because that's what that church did. The Bible says we are the salt and light of the earth. All of us are supposed to be seasoning. Let me be Lawry's. You be lemon pepper. You be pepper. You be cinnamon. You be whatever, but all of us are supposed to let our light shine. Just because mine may shine bright in this area doesn't mean yours shines any less.

Moving from "church hurt" to serving in ministry again . . .

It didn't happen overnight. For the past five years, I have volunteered in ministry at my new church in a surface nature. The ministries I've always been drawn to are youth ministry and college ministry. I love young people. I went to school to be of service to young people. I believe when you're older, even if it's by a few years, you have an obligation to help those who are coming after you. So when my current church hired someone to [lead the youth and college ministries], I saw someone with a heart for working in the areas where I used to. And he wanted to partner in the work [in a genuine way]. I didn't have that [at my former church], so there were times I was asked to get involved and I felt, I'm supposed to be serving but I can't because it's the honeymoon phase. They're going to be nice to me now, and then they're going to use me. If I get involved, I'll start sharing ideas. I'll start working but eventually . . . they're going to start talking about me. It's just going to be just hell for me.

I think what changed was that I started to have people genuinely say, "I need you here. Not only do I need you here, I want you here." Even when I pushed away, "I want you here." When my dad passed, I felt, based on what my dad taught me, that I was supposed to be serving. I started praying more. It seems cliché, but I didn't just pray to God. I wanted to talk to both my earthly father and my Heavenly Father and say, "Help me. I don't want my progress to be halted because of their ignorance." I don't even think they realize what they had. They played me.

Something else changed in me when the minister's wife who caused me all the hell at that church became the First Lady of the church I grew up in. She and her husband lead my home church now. I actually stayed away from my home church, stayed away from going to see my mom and my grandma and other women who shaped me as a young girl because of that person. That's when I knew I had to change. "Church hurt" should not stop you from your relationship with God. God never hurt me. It was the people who said that they knew God and they were being led by God who did. It's hard to understand why he would allow that, but it even has it in the Bible. Everything that happens for you, or that God allows to happen that affects you does not have to be for your detriment. God didn't let that chaos destroy me because I know it would have destroyed somebody else. God strengthened me, and now I feel compelled to be what I needed to someone else at that age.

Closing thoughts on churches seeking to engage millennials who have may have experienced "church hurt" . . .

I would say take the time to talk to people versus talking at them. I would say to take an assessment of the makeup, the design of your church, your ministries, and not just *say* you're approachable but *be* approachable. Be open to accept people. I guess it's meeting them where they are. Don't assume because I am younger in age that I lack knowledge. But don't assume that if I have accomplished a lot that I don't still need to be taught and nurtured by the elders.

Church business can sometimes be bad business. I've seen the ugly side of it, the very ugly side and that can be a major factor in "church hurt." But if I think about the story of Peter and Jesus on the water; regardless of how far out of his grace that I have fallen, I still know his voice. I still hear him calling me. That's what happened to me. As much as I pushed away from the church, and as much as churches can inflict pain that causes others to push away—when you know God, there is something innate that will say "I'm supposed to be doing more for God." Now it may not mean a return to the church they came from, the church that churched them. But eventually, if they know God, they will find a way back to serving in their purpose.

Walking on Water

1. What do you imagine people associate with the "agenda" of your church? (Be realistic in your assessment.) Is this consistent with the message your church body seeks to project? Why or why not?

2. How would you assess the transparency of your congregation's internal operations? What are some ways your congregation can be more transparent and build trust among Millennial disciples?

3. Are you aware of incidents where people have been physically, spiritually, or emotionally hurt in your congregation? What themes are at the core of these conflicts? Are these themes tied to God's enduring standard or to church traditions or "-isms" that can be changed?

4. How does your congregation currently keep up with the lives of your congregants? How can your church be more effective in this effort?

5. What are some of the needs of your church's community and the communities where most of your congregants live? What are some practical ways that your church invests in meeting some of these needs?

CHAPTER FIVE

"Come"

> "'Lord, if it's you,' Peter replied, 'tell me to come to you on the water.'
>
> 'Come,' he said. Then Peter got down out of the boat, walked on the water and came toward Jesus."
>
> MATTHEW 14:28-29

The scene in Matthew 14:28-29 is where things get real for Peter and Jesus' dance on the lake. After discerning that there was a chance it truly was Jesus on the water, and hearing from Jesus the call to "come" and try him, Peter gets down out of the boat, walks on the water, and comes toward Jesus! Again, what Peter proposed of Jesus has no precedent and the other disciples likely told him, "You're crazy for going out to that ghost thinking you might actually meet Jesus on the water!" But there is something about the relationship Peter has cultivated with Christ to this point that not only leads him to respond to Jesus' call, but to feel safe enough to literally risk his life to have an encounter with Jesus on the lake. For me, verse 29 illustrates one of the key elements for black Millennials choosing to engage in their spiritual formation process in various contexts—the creation of safe space.

Safe space is a major concept that is thrown around in different circles and has different connotations based on the context in which it is used. In our case as the church, the creation of safe space is the cultivation of physical, emotional, intellectual, and theological places of engagement where principles can be explored, explained, and even expelled without silencing or devaluing the experience or personhood of those within the community. In a world of increasing cultural, economic, racial, religious, and sexual diversity, safe space is an invaluable quality for any organization or congregation seeking to effectively minister to the souls of black Millennials. There are many elements that contribute to the creation of safe space. We will discuss a few as the chapter continues. Peter and Jesus demonstrate that the cultivation of a trusting relationship is at the core of building safe space.

Reaching Through Relationship

Let's look again at Matthew 14. Peter dreams big and makes an unconventional, if not impossible, request when laying out his terms of engagement with Jesus on the lake: "Lord, if it's you, tell me to come to you on the water." Again, Peter risks his life on what the disciples may have seen as a suicidal-spiritual stunt that could have ended disastrously for him, all because he was confident in the power and presence of Jesus. This kind of trust and confidence is not developed by happenstance or through a casual knowledge of someone. This kind of confidence is cultivated through a meaningful relationship that reveals the capabilities of one another. Peter can trust Jesus because of the ways that Jesus has invested in him and empowered him throughout their relationship.

Matthew's Gospel shows that Jesus spends significant portions of his ministry investing in Peter and the other disciples. After being called by Jesus to be his disciple, Peter gets a front-row seat to Jesus' healing ministry, his teachings, and several demonstrations of his power. He can confirm that Jesus is "the real deal" not simply because of stories he's heard, but because of the access he has been granted by Jesus—the many "meetings after the meeting" when Jesus explains what he has said or done—and the kind of knowledge of Jesus that one could only get by traveling and living alongside him every day for years. Jesus not only invests in Peter through his teachings, but he is also willing to empower Peter. Matthew 10:1 testifies that Jesus empowers Peter with the "authority to drive out impure spirits and to heal every disease and sickness." This combination of investment and empowerment that is cultivated in Peter's relationship with Jesus makes him feel safe enough to join Jesus even under dangerous and unheard-of conditions.

Congregations seeking to be instrumental in the spiritual formation process of black Millennials need to consider the relational model of Jesus to reach them. Black Millennials are hyper-relational—connected to people, causes, and organizations around the world in ways that were impossible in previous generations. Today's noisy relational landscape makes Millennials wary of the motives and benefits of the people and organizations who approach them each day through advertisements, announcements, and solicitations for help. In this climate, congregations who make requests of Millennials—pay into *our* building fund, participate in *our* ministries, add to *our* numbers—without seeking to build genuine relationships with Millennials are lost causes. It is imperative for congregations to develop a disposition of investment and empowerment toward the young adults we seek to disciple, and to do so without any other agenda than to help them see Jesus! In this way, the Christian church is being called to *agenda-free* relational investment into the lives of the black Millennials we seek to serve. Agenda-free relationship-building with young adults in the church's community elevates the sense of investment and empowerment, and it is the first step in creating the necessary safe space that will lead them to "come."

Part of the Conversation

Matthew 14:28-29 helps to illustrate an additional key to the creation of safe space for black Millennials in their spiritual formation process. Peter feels comfortable conversing with Jesus—asking questions of Jesus and making requests of Jesus. Peter is unafraid that he will be ignored and expects Jesus to answer his inquiries. Somewhere along the journey with Jesus, Peter was made to feel that his voice was valuable and that Jesus would not simply dictate to him, but would engage him in conversation.

My research findings are clear that one of the keys to creating safe space for black Millennials to theologically develop within our congregations is to create spaces where their voices can be heard and are valued. This makes sense when we consider the way that Millennials are given (or have taken) a voice in every other segment of their societal development. Since they were children, Millennials have been given a voice by television networks like Viacom (BET, MTV, Nickelodeon) as they vote for their favorite music artists, movies, and songs on these networks' award shows and platforms. Millennials like DeAndre Cortez "Soulja Boy" Way and Jo-Issa Rae Diop turned to online platforms like YouTube to give them a voice, which eventually led them to be discovered and offered record deals and television production contracts with major labels. Young Millennial writers and thought-leaders do not have to wait to have their ideas picked up by local publications; they can produce, publish, and monetize their own blogs and podcasts to be consumed on a global stage. Social media platforms (for better or worse) have given Millennials the opportunity to express their opinions and thoughts to a worldwide room at any time—even in the Lord's church. For digital natives, the ability to have one's voice be heard is not a luxury but a way of life and an expectation.

Didactically, black Millennials indicated that they desire to be taught in a community of learners where their voices are heard and valued amongst a group of peers. Teaching models that favor the preacher or pastor as the authoritative lecturer will ultimately miss the masses of black Millennials who prefer the teacher to operate as a facilitator of explorative conversation within a community of learners. In this paradigm, the leader who prepares the lesson and is trained in biblical exegesis and cultural scholarship is as much a learner as anyone else in the room—fostering open dialogue where no one's interpretation or insight of the text is dismissed. In many ways, it is a model that harkens to the Jewish tradition of arguing, interpreting, and debating the meaning of the Scriptures within a community. Jesus illustrates this principle when he asks his disciples in Luke 10:26, "What is written in the Law? How do you read it?" Jesus makes space for open dialogue and interpretation among the listening community while skillfully providing correction and direction as needed. This is the challenge and call for congregations seeking to create safe space for the spiritual formation of black Millennials.

A Posture of Compassion

A third element in the creation of safe space for spiritual formation is for leaders and teachers of the Word to intentionally take a posture of compassion. I do not mean compassion that merely says, "Aww, I feel bad for you and want to help you." For me, compassion is accurately defined by Monsignor William McCarthy in his book *The Conspiracy: An Innocent Priest*. McCarthy writes, "Compassion is the quality of being able to get inside the skin of another in order to respond with loving care."[1] While many Christians would like to see the world in black and white, each day black Millennials become more aware of its deep complexities as they live them out. Assumptions that the black church has made about her congregants through the generations—about family structures, appropriate attire, sexual preferences, tastes in music and media, or religious beliefs and backgrounds—are no longer valid, and the dismissal of these complexities as lived out by black Millennials each day will only sour the taste these young adults have for the church and her God.

To be clear, this is not a call to accommodate or affirm everything that this generation holds as normative. As my pastor continues to remind us, Christ has always been countercultural and we do not take our cues from the world. Leaders and congregations must continue to faithfully search for God's heart and speak

God's standards through careful exegesis and prayerful interpretation of the Scriptures. However, it is a call for the church
universal to take a disposition that seeks to get into the skin of
the Peters of this generation as a way to understand the origin
of their theological perspectives. As in the days of Jesus, we will
not always come to the same conclusions on various perspectives, principles, and theological points of view. However, with
an intentional disposition of compassion—constantly seeking to
get into the skin of black Millennials to understand how they
see and understand God and the world—congregations can build
safe spaces where there are disagreements in principles without
the demonization or devaluing of one's personhood.

Welcome to The Brook

During my tenure as the College Minister at Wheeler Avenue
Baptist Church, I have sought to slowly build such a space for
the Millennials in our church. Every Thursday night our college
students and several young adults come together for their own
time of Bible study called "The Brook." The Brook is not a particularly large gathering, but it is one that seeks to foster safe
space for young adults to wrestle theologically. During the course
of my research, we conducted a focus group with them to hear
what elements of the Bible study were essential in creating an
environment that made them willing to engage Jesus on the water.
Prayerfully, leaders, pastors, and teachers can use some of the following feedback as you prayerfully consider programming safe
spaces for this demographic.

No-Judgment Zones

Black Millennials desire a space to engage in theological conversation without feeling "judged" or put down about their personal
views and lifestyles by other members of the congregation (or by
their teachers and leaders). They desire a safe space to engage

the Divine where they can present their authentic selves. They desire safe space to articulate inner wrestling and ask questions that may conflict with theological and doctrinal views held by the congregation. This safe space must take into consideration the varying views and levels of literacy around the Bible. While many black Millennials still revere the Bible as sacred text that is central to their faith development, many do not view the text as infallible. Teachers must be prepared to define their own positions systematically without dismissing the arguments and positions of those who study among the group. These safe spaces are best cultivated through consistency and intimacy (possibly in smaller, intimate groups) and may be aided by techniques that utilize anonymity as a tool for more authentic discussion.

Servant-Leader Self-Disclosure

One of the major factors in the creation of safe space is the transparency and truthfulness of the servant-leader. In Matthew 14, Peter is willing to walk on the water based on his trust in the power and presence of Jesus. He knew Jesus could be trusted because Jesus had been disclosing his true identity to Peter throughout their journey together. Pastors, teachers, and leaders seeking to serve in the spiritual formation process of black Millennials must understand this need for transparency and space for mutual disclosure. Congregations cannot expect their young adults to be willing to pour out their souls and share their struggles, failures, and triumphs without a level of transparency and mutual disclosure from their servant-leaders. This truth and transparency helps to take the leader off the pedestal of absolute authority and pious perfection and helps position them within the community of learners.

To be sure, this is risky business for servant-leaders who are called to minister to black Millennials. Creating a culture of transparency from the top down means leaving the leadership open for tough questions and accountability from the young disciples in the community. It may also mean exposing the reality that we as leaders do not have all the answers or that we have our own unresolved theological questions. But it is a necessity in restoring this generation's trust in the Christian church and her leadership—a prerequisite for Peter to step out of the boat and walk toward us.

VALUABLE VOICES

Featured Millennial: Nichole, age 22, Graduating college student and frequent participant at The Brook

On the challenges of the "community of learners," open-discussion model . . .

Some of the trouble I have with the open discussion is . . . when people kind of go left, and by left meaning either going against Scripture or speaking out . . . about how they feel about taboo things in the church, as far as drugs, sex, money, and things like that. When people go left in that area—where they feel like it's okay to have premarital sex, they feel like it makes sense [to say], "Oh, I need to get drunk" or "I need to get high to speak to God, or be at one with the Lord"—when it comes to things like that, and there's no [immediate] correction provided, I feel like that poses an issue, because when it hangs in the air like that and nobody corrects it . . . personally I feel like I talk enough. I talk enough for everybody.

When it comes from you [as a leader], I feel like it's better received. Or even if you're confirming what someone else has said, it's definitely better received by The Brook. But when it hangs in the air like that, I feel like maybe people around them, who may be feeling the same way but weren't transparent enough to come out and want to say it themselves, they may feel confirmed in what they're doing. So they may feel like, "Well, she does this, that, and a third and Rev. didn't say anything about it, so it must be okay." And even if someone in The Brook says something to clarify or correct, maybe pertaining to Scripture, they may take that with a grain of salt because it's like, "Okay, they're my age," or, "They're on my level, that's my peer. Therefore, I can take what they're saying with a grain of salt," compared to if you were to say something.

Suggestions to strengthen the "community of learners" model . . .

My suggestion would be, I feel like I find that the same things come up. The same things, really because of the age group we're in, it's always either about drinking, drugs, or sex. 'Cause you know, that's all these college kids think about. I think what may be beneficial moving forward is to maybe have an arsenal of book-chapter-verse that you can use in those situations. Because I know how you were saying you don't want to speak on something and you don't have that context to back it up. You can say this, but students are looking for answers and don't want to walk away confused without an answer because you're not ready to back it up with Scripture.

So maybe just having an arsenal of Scripture for those three subjects, because I feel like those are the ones that come up the most. Every time we go through Sex, Snapchat, and Soul Ties, it's somebody coming out the woodworks, making everybody think it's okay to have premarital sex. And we all know that's dead.

Walking on Water

1. What are some of the areas of your ministry where Millennials are invited to lend their voices to the conversation?

2. How can you create no-judgment zones in your congregation? Are there spaces where this is already happening?

3. Who are some of the members of your congregation that you need to get into the skin of? What are your assumptions about them? How can your community intentionally make them feel welcomed at your church?

4. As a leader or teacher, how transparent are you about the victories and struggles you have lived through? What influences your current level of transparency? What are your fears?

Notes

1. Monsignor William McCarthy, *The Conspiracy: An Innocent Priest* (Indiana: iUniverse Publishing, 2010), 71.

CHAPTER SIX

"When He Saw the Wind"

"But when he saw the wind, he was afraid and, beginning to sink, cried out, 'Lord, save me!'"

MATTHEW 14:30

Emboldened by the trust and safe space that Peter finds in Christ, he takes a major risk and comes down out of the boat. It is a risk, however, that he soon finds is worthwhile! Peter initially dips his toe into the lake and finds that somehow the lucid watery surface he was accustomed to has been replaced by a sturdy, solid platform. He decides to plant both of his feet down and, to his surprise, he is *standing* on the lake. *This is incredible!* he thinks, because even though he asked to engage Christ in this way, there was still some doubt that it would happen. Yet there he is—first standing and now walking closer and closer to Christ on this lake of impossibility. *This is amazing!*, Peter thinks as he watches the sea creatures scurrying in the waters beneath his feet. The brothers whom Peter left in the boat are getting farther away as he moves closer to the Messiah. Everything is great!

Until suddenly, a violent gust of wind blows across the lake—creating waves and causing small pieces of debris to fly through the air with aimless fury. The sound of the wind is enough to startle

Peter, but the scene he sees unfolding in front of him is even more terrifying. As he watches the manifestation of the power of the wind on the water, he feels himself beginning to lose leverage and traction beneath his feet. What was once a solid watery platform beneath him has given way to the lake's original form, and he realizes that he's sinking. What a turn of events! What started out as a promising dance with Jesus is now a sea of second thoughts—not because of anything Jesus himself has done, but because of what Peter sees and experiences as he walks ever closer to Christ.

The situation that Peter faces when he is frightened on the lake with Jesus has important parallels to the spiritual formation journeys of many black Millennials who have sought to engage the church's call. For many, the initial worship experiences, Bible studies, or encounters with Christ that encourage them to give congregations a try are exciting and exhilarating. Like Peter, they muster the courage to engage the "ghost"—finding just enough safe space to risk being hurt or wasting their time. In the beginning, things are just fine. They see themselves getting closer to Jesus; they are doing, feeling, and experiencing things in themselves that they never imagined; they are excited by the opportunity that Christ has invited them to. However, at some point in their walk toward Christ they begin to see things that scare them—environmental elements outside of the boat that are not a product of the Jesus they seek to get close to, but are happening around where they expect him to be. They begin to see things within the church of Christ and in the Bible that frighten them and help sink their faith-filled walks toward Christ.

During my study, five major impediments surfaced as terrifying winds in the lives of our Millennial Peters: ageism, hypocrisy, unexplained inconsistencies, lack of community and cultural engagement, and issues around sexuality. While this list is not exhaustive, congregations who wrestle with these impediments to engage black Millennials will be further along in the process of becoming attractive centers of spiritual formation for the next generation.

Ageism

Let us start with ageism. One of the Valuable Voices in this book features Rev. Verdell A. Wright, who began his interview talking about the notion of ageism and how it is one of the key impediments to Millennials participating in the life of churches around the country. "Black Millennials at this stage of our development are not children," Wright reflected. He is correct. The youngest of the Millennials (born in the year 2000) are, at the time of this writing, entering their senior year of high school. At this point most black Millennials are adults—working *adult* jobs, making *adult* decisions, having *adult* families, raising children, getting married, and making *adult* money. Yet in congregations across the nation where black Millennials are participating in worship and fellowship, there is still subtle messaging and an ethic that suggests that young black Millennials are children. There's no doubt that churches want Millennials to engage in the work of the church and to contribute to the church through their tithes and their offerings, but the feeling among many black Millennials is that they are viewed as cute novelties at best. The unfortunate reality is this: if the church as an institution is to survive the religious shifts of the next few decades, she cannot afford to view Millennials as a special project, but must engage them as available partners to the life and work of the church today!

As previously discussed, it is crucial for congregations to follow Jesus' model of building a meaningful and mutually beneficial relationship with Peter prior to bidding him to come. Prior to his invitation to engage him in what *he* was doing out there on the water, Jesus took the time to invest and to empower Peter. Jesus took time to invest in Peter through the teachings that Jesus provided after calling Peter and his brother Andrew to become fishers of people. He took the time to invest in Peter as they traveled and talked together each day of his journey—with Peter picking up spiritual nuggets that the average person who followed Jesus may not have had access to. But Jesus also empowered Peter. The

Bible says that he empowered Peter and the disciples with the ability to cast out demons, heal the sick, and perform miracles in the name of Jesus (Matthew 10:1). He gave Peter the opportunity to do some of the vital and transformative work that people expected from an encounter with Christ.

Congregations must follow Jesus' lead if we are serious about increasing the participation of black Millennials in the work of the church. We must continue to invest in them—finding ways to invest in their academic, familial, occupational, and educational well-being while tending to the needs of their spirits through our teaching and preaching. We must also empower them to be a part of the ministry of Jesus Christ before we make demands of them to come out on the water and do what we want them to do. This means creating spaces for Millennials to participate as leaders in the church today! When I consult with church leaders, it troubles me when congregations want Millennials to be involved in the work of the church, but are not willing to allow them to lead in any capacity. The irony is that black Millennials are CEOs and founders of some of the biggest corporations in the country. Away from the sanctuary, these young people operate as trial lawyers, businesswomen, entrepreneurs, CEOs, principals, and teachers. They are politicians, doctors, and engineers—people who are doing great things, making major money, and making major decisions in their fields. Yet when it comes to the church they are somehow incapable of being a suitable deacon or trustee.

How are Millennials who balance budgets for multimillion-dollar corporations not qualified to be trustees of a small congregation because they're not old enough or did not grow up in that church? How is it that those who love God and serve well in other capacities are somehow too young to serve as deacons or ministry leaders? Why can't the black Millennials in our congregation who host podcasts or do multimedia work in graphic design and videography assist in creating modernized church media (announcements, flyers, etc.) or help improve the church's use of technology? It is time for the Christian church, if it wants to engage black Millennials, to rid herself of ageism and position these adults to lead.

To be sure, there are those who will critique and push the other side of the ageism conversation. Many congregational leaders believe that Millennials are impulsive, are hard to work with, and do not have enough respect or desire to honor some of the long-standing traditions of the church. To some degree this is true. Millennials do have issues with patience and time, primarily because they operate in a society that does not require them to wait for anything that they want to happen. Remember, this is the *American Idol* generation where stars can be created in 12 weeks and are offered multimillion-dollar contracts. This is the generation that does not have to wait to begin leading in a business; they can create their own. They do not have to wait for somebody to offer them a platform; they can utilize digital technologies to create platforms for themselves, such as through blogs or YouTube.

No, Millennials are not accustomed to "waiting their turn." There is indeed impatience within the generation, and black Millennials (through meaningful relationship) must also be encouraged to honor their ancestors, honor important traditions, and be engaged in the work of the church in intergenerational ways. However, the church cannot continue to allow the next generation of church leaders to walk away from the church because they have the capacity, skill, and heart to serve but are not empowered by the power brokers, stakeholders, and gatekeepers of our local congregations.

Scandal and Hypocrisy

A second impediment identified by black Millennials surrounds the scandal and hypocrisy they experience in the church. Adam Hamilton, author of *When Christians Get It Wrong*,[1] outlines several areas of faith and practice in the Christian church that turn young people away. The very first area that Hamilton highlights in the book is "When Christians Are Unchristian."[2]

Hamilton provides commentary on young people turning away from the faith because of the hypocrisy they see and the wrongs committed in the name of Christ or by those who claim to be Christian. Highly publicized pastoral scandals, extravagant lifestyles of church leaders on television, mismanagement of church finances, and outright abuse in the black church have created a great mistrust of the church in the hearts of many black Millennials. Congregations must be intentional about creating systems of accountability and seek to earnestly live out the message that is proclaimed and taught in that sacred space. As genuine faith and earnest institutional integrity are displayed, it will prayerfully cause black Millennials debating whether to step out of their boats to say, "This is a church that means what it says and puts words into action."

With this said, I know full well that there is no such thing as a perfect church. There's no such thing as perfect leaders, perfect pastors, or perfect preachers. I would argue that it may be impossible to live this Christian faith without *some* level of hypocrisy. In fact, I sit in Pastor Paul's "Amen corner" every time I read his words in Romans 7:21 (NLT): "I have discovered this principle of life—that when I want to do what is right, I inevitably do what is wrong." This is not a call for the church to somehow transform into "super saints" who never sin or never get things wrong. Rather, this is an invitation for congregations to consider how the Body of Christ can hold itself, its leaders, and its members accountable so that the abuse, misuse, and unchristian conduct that hurts too many seeking to engage the church are not continuously being swept under a rug. When those who claim the name of Christ are wrong or hurtful, the church has a responsibility to quickly say, "We don't endorse or condone this behavior. While we're a place that strives to live like Christ in grace, love, and forgiveness, we are also a place that believes in accountability and attempting to walk out the tenets of our faith."

VALUABLE VOICES

Featured Millennial: Peyton Morris, age 31, Personal banker, Dallas, TX

On her upbringing in the church . . .

I am the oldest of three. I'm the only girl and we were in church all my life. Since I was born, I was always in the church. I started singing in the church choir when I was five. I was on the usher board. I was a part of the youth ministry. Now, as a young adult, I was a part of the young adult choir at my church, and I was also a part of the young adult ministry. My dad, he's the pastor of a small church locally here, and I was pretty active in his church, helping out with some of the young teenage girls and also on the praise ministry [before relocating to another church]. In my current church, I was heavily involved in the young adult choir until I stepped down recently.

On leaving the music ministry and taking a step back from the church . . .

For one, I was working on my master's degree, so part of it was time management. It was hard committing to a ministry with work and school. I'm in a sorority, so it was hard balancing everything. But I also started questioning the church, and there were a lot of things that I saw that I didn't necessarily agree with, particularly in the young adult choir that I was a part of. There were also some things I was participating [in] that I wasn't proud of personally. I prayed about it, and I thought that the best choice for me was to step down and focus solely on my walk with Christ versus the ministry of the church.

There were several occasions where I saw individuals who were singled out because they were different. There were clique-ish things—but I think that you find that in any institution, not just the church. It's unfortunate but I saw a lot of clique-ish things, a lot of homosexuality, and sexual sin. That was a little different, and I feel like if we are the church we're supposed to be addressing those issues and helping people repent for their sinful acts. Rather than doing that, it was almost as if we were pacifying and saying it's "okay" because we would rather increase our numbers than rectify a situation that's not a godly situation. From the leadership to the actual choir members, people just weren't living Christ-like lives and it just didn't seem like a genuine ministry.

In terms of me stepping away from the church for a while, I think people get wrapped up in what they see *at* church versus living as though you *are* the church. I know the Bible tells us to go to church so that we can fellowship with people of like mind, but when I looked at the actual institution of church or church as an institution, it's just a lot of hypocrisy and things that don't line up with what the Word of God says. For me, going to church and still partici-pating in church when all of that is taking place, it's almost as if I'm condoning that behavior in the church and [I] felt I needed to remove myself. It was starting to affect me and I even found myself taking place in some of those same carnal behaviors and doing things that the Bible tells you you're not supposed to do. Yeah, it was a turn-off.

Suggestions for churches looking to engage black Millennials . . .

I think they shouldn't be so concerned with the numbers. I feel like pastors and leaders have to practice what they stand for. Rather than playing a numbers game, worried about offending someone, I feel like you should speak truth in love and help people understand when we are out of line. We're all sinners. We all fall short. At the same time, if you're actively practicing the sin, and you're not actively trying to change that behavior, then that's not right. If you're not striving towards being the Christian that you're supposed to be, I feel like leadership should step in. When people in the church are practicing sin, it needs to be addressed. I am *not* saying it should be done the way churches did in the "old days" when you had to come before the church and tell the church you sinned. I've actually been a part of a church where that took place, and that was a turn-off too. But the church can't be afraid to address things and not worry about whether or not someone is going to leave the church and decrease the numbers. At the end of the day, reproof and correction are also tenets of the church and we have a responsibility to help individuals realize when they are out of step with the Word of God.

Inconsistencies and Interpretation

I'll never forget being asked the question by a young adult one day after Bible study, "How did Judas die?" Later I found out that this young adult was confused about the death of Judas because in Matthew 27, Judas hangs himself on a tree. Yet in Acts 1:18, Luke writes that Judas dies from falling headlong into a field, where his body bursts open. This Millennial's question was, "Which one is it, and why are there two versions of Judas's death in a Bible that we claim to be the inerrant, infallible word of God?" Did Judas die twice? Did Judas hang himself first, but the rope wasn't strong enough so his body fell to the ground and burst open? Or does the Bible contradict itself? Tough question. I later explained to him the complex way that the Gospel narratives were formed—that these Gospels were created several years after the death of Christ, primarily by authors who were disciples of Christ's disciples. Over time, pseudonyms were given to these Gospel writers to honor the tradition that the story came out of. I concluded that there may seemingly be discrepancies in the way that the story is told due to time, tradition, and translation. However, what is important is what is happening at the heart of the gospel and the heart of the teaching of the text.

This answer seemed to satisfy this young adult, but it is risky (if not cringeworthy) business for some teachers of the text. Too many times there is a fear in the black church that if we are transparent, open, and honest about the way in which we get our texts and some of our traditions, it will cause confusion or repel people from the church. For those who have been theologically trained in a seminary or Bible college, there seems to be a fear that presenting what is learned in a seminary would only confuse people and cause people to walk away from the faith. I would argue that if the church is *not* willing to address and help young people properly interpret the perceived inconsistencies in the text and in the traditions of the church, black Millennials will continue to walk away. We must risk turning our Sunday schools into seminaries in order to continue to be a part of the spiritual formation process of black Millennials. This puts the onus on leaders in the church to take seriously the need to be theologically educated. Theological education is *not* optional for this generation of church leaders who seek to serve black Millennials. There is a necessity for preachers, teachers, and leaders of this generation to be educated and aware of church history, systematic theology, the Old Testament, the New Testament, and biblical languages to ensure that we can respond to the questions that black Millennials have around the perceived inconsistencies in our sacred texts and our sacred traditions.

Lack of Cultural and Community Engagement

I'll never forget a phone call I received in the summer of 2015. I was preaching a revival in Oklahoma City and my host took me to visit the Oklahoma City Memorial Museum. While going through the museum, I received a phone call from a friend who serves as a campus minister at Texas Southern University. She was calling to inform me that several members of her college ministry decided to walk away from both her church and her campus ministry. When I asked their reason for walking away, her answer was heartbreaking but helpful to our conversation. Their reason for walking away revolved around Sandra Bland, a young woman who had just received a job at Prairie View A&M and was taken into a Waller County jail less than an hour away from TSU's campus and never came out. As suspicion of police misconduct continued to rise, the students watched this ordeal unfold, waiting for my friend's church to *do* something. Ultimately, they decided to leave her church (and eventually Christianity altogether) because they felt that the church had done nothing to address what was happening right in the church's backyard. For them, the church had been silent in its response—there were no marches, no protests, no provisions made to help those who would be on the ground trying to make a change in the wake of Sandra Bland's death.

I later discovered that my friend's church had indeed made efforts to help the case of Sandra Bland and to support the student body of Prairie View A&M, but these conversations were occurring behind the scenes between the pastor and school officials. The congregation was never made aware of how their church was engaged in the hunt for justice for another slain black life. My critique to the leadership of that church was that while they were doing some things behind the scenes, black Millennials of the church could not *see* what the church was doing. For a generation raised on pixels and video clips, it is not enough for churches to say from the pulpit that they support the work of justice or efforts in the community. Black Millennials must *see* us in action, and churches must utilize media and marketing to tell and show our stories. If a church cannot show what she is doing to be engaged in eradicating cultural and community ills, particularly those in the black community, it is not a church that will ultimately hold weight among black Millennials.

My study found that the murder of Trayvon Martin, which many saw as the genesis of the Black Lives Matter movement, was one of the top three life markers for black Millennials. For black Millennials, there is a sense of activism and a desire to be a part of social change in the sphere of justice and quality of life for people of color. The congregations who will remain relevant among black Millennials are the congregations who win souls while engaging in community activism and organizing, public policy reform, and social justice initiatives that increase the vitality of black and brown life. These congregations are unafraid to speak from the pulpit against social injustices committed in the lives of black and brown people—churches invested in and working for the good of the communities where they are planted.

VALUABLE VOICES

Featured Millennial: Rev. Sammie J. Dow, age 30, Millennial preacher/pastor with traditional roots, Former National Director for Youth for the NAACP

On a contemporary church model that embraces the importance of Afrocentricity . . .

One of the things I think traditional African American congregations are struggling with is this notion of feeling like we have to "de-blacken" the black church experience. There have been many articles that speak to the desire for Millennials to have a contemporary, progressive, efficient worship experience—but not lose what are the traits, the DNA, the pillars of the African American worship experience. I think that as churches look at what their approaches will be to modernizing their worship experiences and program offerings, we also have to look at the importance of helping Millennials specifically identify themselves in faith. I think we also have to have hard conversations about church history, Christian history, roots of faith, and really helping people understand the totality of what is written in the biblical text as it relates to faith and justice. We also have to address some of the oppressive theologies we've preached and taught over the years so that we can see the emergence of a progressive, Afrocentric, twenty-first-century theology that is inclusive, that is diverse, that is rooted in an ethic of love, but also centered on the need to stand on the side of the marginalized and the oppressed.

Practical steps to help churches mobilize and engage in community work . . . .

One of the things that I think the church has to realize is each church has a very unique role and function to play in the larger movement. Every church is not meant to be a church on the streets protesting. Every church is not meant to be the church that is consistently advocating, or in the press, or in the news. Everyone has a lane that we all have to run, so the first step in churches wanting to engage the justice work that we must engage is identifying our lane. Once you identify your lane, you have to unapologetically run in your lane. The challenge we have is when churches attempt to run across multiple lanes. They end up not running in any lane effectively. So, the first step is identifying your lane and being unapologetic about, "This is who we are. This is the lane we've decided run in to do the work."

Now, as I'm running in my lane, I also have to recognize the importance of partnering with folks who are running in different lanes so that we create a community-wide, comprehensive, holistic strategy for how African American churches and faith-based institutions and organizations in our city and our region are going to collaborate to move the work forward. That's step number one. If Church A is to be the church that is centrally focused on direct services—what we would call charity work—run in that lane and do it well, because other churches in your area will be positioned to do more of the social protests and social organizing work. That's very necessary, but so is what we would consider the "charity work," the direct service provision in cities. That work is very much necessary, just as the more macro systemic work that has to happen. So, number one, identify your lane and unapologetically run in your lane.

Don't negate or underestimate the importance of training. Millennials want to do this work. Most just don't know where to start. The protests, the marches, the rallies, and the things that we see—those are effective and those have a place in the movement, but we've also got to teach young people what authentic and true advocacy looks like beyond just protest. Protest is not a strategy; it's a tactic. We've got to give young people a comprehensive view of what organizing in communities looks like, with the ultimate recognition that if we're not organizing people electorally, all of our efforts are mute. We've got to organize people to the polls to ultimately change and shift who the decision-makers are, because that ultimately impacts the policies that we've been advocating for or against on the back end.

Number two, look at comprehensive training strategies. For me, I came from the white, progressive organizing space prior to transitioning into ministry—institutions such as the New Organizing Institute or the Midwest Academy, which is, probably in white progressive spaces, one of the more prominent organizing institutions. Figure out curriculums there that work, and tailor them to your context because ultimately we're all trying to push forward the same goals. We just have different audiences that we're working with. Pull from the Midwest Academy training. Send groups of your young people to Midwest Academy trainings so that they learn the fundamentals of organizing because that's what's critically necessary.

Finally, I would say to be willing to step in wherever the community says it needs you. One of the things that churches oftentimes do is we create the prescription before we understand what the diagnosis is. We've got to be willing to go into communities and spend time on the ground listening. Working with community members. Lifting their voices as the central voices in the conversation, and then saying, "This is what the community says it wants, it needs, it wants to see. Here's how we've worked with them to develop a plan. We've now deployed this army of folks from our congregation that have been trained who are now going to train the community so that we create a grassroots coalition of folks pulling the work forward."

Recap: Identify your lane, run in your lane, and be unapologetic about it. Secondly, we have to invest in training people to do this work. This isn't something that happens by osmosis. Then lastly, make sure that you are coming from a community-based perspective, and you've spent time on the ground in the trenches with people so that whatever you produce, it looks like, it smells like, it feels like the community that you're in.

The Ebony Elephant

Finally, the last major impediment relates to the black church's relationship to the LGBTQ community. Even as the church seeks to create community with those in the Black Lives Matter movement, one of the greatest critiques from the Black Lives Matter movement revolves around the black church's treatment of the LGBTQ community. Many young leaders continue to express frustration that while the black church professes to understand race and to fight for the lives of black people as a whole, the church seems to have a change of mind as it relates to members of the black community who identify as LGBTQ. Obviously there are theological reasons for this tension that must be considered, and we will explore them more in the following chapter. However, black churches who are not willing to have serious conversations around their theology and ethics on human sexuality are not black churches who will survive the shift as it relates to spiritual formation choices for black Millennials.

VALUABLE VOICES

Featured Millennial: Rev. Verdell A. Wright, age 33, Licensed Clergy, PhD Student, Washington, DC

On the importance of reconsidering grounding theological premises . . .

Before we even get to [conversations around spirituality and sexuality]—because I think those things are important—I think we have to consider our theology, period. We have to consider where our theology comes from. I think with the prosperity gospel, we have allowed the idea of prosperity to hijack what is good about black faith. I think we have to step back and think about the things that we are believing and what we are saying. If you look at what preachers and pastors have been saying from the '70s and '80s onward, and then look at what some others are saying before then—not that it was all perfect—but it was different; particularly when we think of the black church and this triumphant, social justice/ civil rights movement. When we think of that picture and you hear what those folks are saying and then hear what some of our folks are saying from the pulpit today—it's not the same. And it's not just a function of, "Well, those were different times." It's a function of somehow becoming imbued with these TBN [Trinity Broadcast Network] aspirations and this prosperity gospel—underlying things and [a mindset of] "I think it and it is. Boom. Pow. Name it, claim it." A lot of us do that in a lighter way. I think we have to really sit with that and see how we've really gone in a different direction than our ancestors. It's not just about going to seminary and hav-ing these big books. It's about acknowledging that this is not a faith that our ancestors themselves would have held. This is a departure from what that is because the prosperity gospel does not affirm life, flesh, and body. It's hard to talk about civil rights and treating human people well if you think that material doesn't matter unless it's cars and houses.

I think we also have to honestly question our theodicy. I don't think that we've done a good job, overall, with being honest about the questions of faith. And I get that because I think, for me, when you understand how people have used faith, particularly African Americans, it's about God "making a way out of no way," and "We have to make it through," and "God's going to do it," and "God's going to rescue us." That can be the only anchor of hope people have, so I understand that. I don't want to demean that. I think the important part, though, is to address that in the twenty-first century, everyone's prayers do not get answered. I'm sure there is someone holy in Flint. I'm sure there is, but they don't have any water! I'm sure that there are plenty of people who meet all the requirements of righteousness, "holy living" if you will, and they are destroyed by our world and apparently ignored by God. Instead of trying to figure out little pat answers to excuse that, we have to allow people to sit with their questions.

We have to allow a bigger space for theological questions, for theological anger. How do you, in a post–Civil Rights moment when Donald Trump is president after everything that God apparently "delivered" us from, how do you make sense of his election theologically with all of the things that he has said and done during and after his campaign? You have to have an answer for that because I thought God was on the winning side, so did God leave? What happened? I think we have to allow that question to be set with an answer in a more honest way than "God will do it."

I think doing those two things will allow us to have a more honest conversation about gender and sexuality, because those things undergird so much of why we think the way that we do about those two aspects that if we don't address how we understand theology and we don't understand how we address God's "goodness" in the world, then we won't understand—we won't be able to even entertain the conversation of, "Well, this little girl is gay and that's good because God created her good."

We can't even have that if we're not willing to open up for those other possibilities. I think that [we need] to really sit with what we believe and why we believe it and to look toward some of our own figures of faith to see what they thought, and I think if we looked really far back, we'd find some surprising things that we probably wouldn't have thought existed. When we examine what some AME folks thought about prayer or God or what we should do, we would be surprised at some of the things that they actually thought. It's a million miles away from what we would say today, but we think that it's not. I think that needs to be there.

Walking on Water

1. What are some of the areas of ministry where you can (and should) empower more qualified young leaders to serve?

2. How do you as a church or ministry hold leaders accountable for behavior that is abusive or contrary to the will and witness of Christ?

3. What are some areas of theological education necessary to equip your teachers and leaders to answer the tough questions black Millennials may ask about the Bible and church history?

4. What is your church's lane in service to your community? What training opportunities might you need to consider for your young leaders?

5. What is your church's theology and ethic relating to the black LGBTQ community? When do you have conversations around spirituality and sexuality?

Notes

1. Adam Hamilton, *When Christians Get It Wrong* (Nashville: Abingdon Press, 2013), Kindle Edition.

2. Ibid., Loc. 69.

CHAPTER SEVEN

"Why Did You Doubt?"

"Immediately Jesus reached out his hand and caught him. 'You of little faith,' he said, 'why did you doubt?'"

MATTHEW 14:31

As Peter is sinking in the middle of the stormy lake—distracted and frightened by the windy elements in the environment around Jesus—he makes a wise decision. Refusing to suffer and sink in silence, Peter cries, "Lord, save me!" Moved with compassion and care for his disciple, Jesus stretches out his hand and grabs Peter before he is fully submerged in the deep. As Jesus pulls him up, quietly restoring Peter's peace, it is Jesus who is now ready to speak. "You of little faith," Jesus says. Can't you see that you had the opportunity to have an encounter with me that few others have dared to *dream* about? Peter—the one who has walked closest to me since the beginning of my ministry and who will ultimately be tasked with leading this ministry when I am gone— "why did you doubt?"

Most interpretations of this text focus on the part of Jesus' question where he seemingly is chastising his disciple for a lack of faith. In truth, it is the job of the Body of Christ and its leadership to occasionally make assessments of the faith lived out by our congregants. Yet what is more instructive for our purposes is the "b" clause of the question: "why did you doubt?" It is both significant and instructive that Jesus, whom Peter seeks to engage in a new way on the water, takes the time to create space to hear about Peter's doubts and concerns. Jesus' question to Peter skips over the obvious environmental elements that Peter *sees* that invokes his feet-sinking fear, and instead engages Peter around what he *feels* and *thinks*. As churches and congregations seek to be effective partners in the spiritual formation process of black Millennials, we too must be willing to make space to hear about the sources of doubt and the thoughts of the generation we seek to disciple.

During the course of my study, we were able to investigate the doubts that black Millennials have around the Christian church and Christ's teachings. We also asked questions to discern the themes or ideas that black Millennials most sought the church to teach about and have conversations around. In the following pages, I will highlight the most prominent areas of discussion and teaching that black Millennials desire the church to engage, then address four major areas of doubt for black Millennials as they relate to the teachings of the church.

Deal with It, Reverend!

One of the questions survey participants were asked during our study was "Which subject matters have you experienced or discussed in the teaching ministries of your church that have been most helpful?" While wading through the answers of hundreds of respondents, three subjects appeared most frequently. The two most frequent responses surrounded walking in faith and trusting God's plan for their lives. Many black Millennials are navigating unstable job markets (despite their high levels of education and proficiency), gentrification, exorbitant living costs, and the craziness of love and relationships. In such a world, it is important for these young adults to know that God indeed has plans for them, and for them to be given the tools to forge ahead in faith in God until they begin to see what they are expecting by faith. To this end, black Millennials found teachings on discipleship, spiritual disciplines, and basic essentials to Christian living to be most helpful in their development processes. The third response related to teachings on relationships—and not simply relationship series with a romantic or spousal focus. What these study participants found most helpful in their spiritual formation process were teachings on healthy relationships with family and friends, finding a spouse, preparing for marriage, and sexuality.

We also asked our study participants, "What subject matters are you most interested in being addressed in the teaching ministries of your church?" Black Millennials expressed that they were most interested in engaging studies on how to grow through spiritual stagnation. Many expressed a heart to grow in God but felt they lacked the tools to engage God at a "deeper level." As a part of this conversation around spiritual growth, black Millennials also expressed a heartfelt desire to discern the voice of God in their lives. Questions such as "How does God speak?" or "How am I sure when it's my ambition or God's voice?" were all mentioned as a part of a foremost desire to grow spiritually.

Second, participants expressed an interest in discussing dating and relationships, as well as a desire for the church to address numerous questions around sexuality (such as sexual purity, sex before marriage, and sexual orientation). Lessons that address questions like "What is the nature of Christian dating?" or "What are the qualities we should be looking for in a potential spouse?" or "What is the difference between courtship and dating?" or "What boundaries should be employed in Christian dating?" would be appreciated.

Third, black Millennials expressed a strong interest in teachings that would address issues at the intersection of spirituality and social justice. Where should the Christian church stand in matters of discrimination and oppression, and what should the church *do* in response to the injustices experienced in black and brown communities around the world? What role should people of faith have in government and public policy? Where would

Jesus be situated in the midst of the Black Lives Matter movement or in response to the Dakota Access Pipeline issue? Congregations who intentionally display to black Millennials a desire to "stay woke"—fearlessly and *frequently* engaging in teaching and conversation at the intersection of faith, racial identity, and social justice—model a prophetic witness that echoes in the hearts of this emerging generation.

Dealing with Doubts

Today's Peters most desire for congregations to help provide guidance and answers in the relations that matter most to them—their relationship with God, their romantic and familial relationships, and with regards to racial relations and injustice. Congregations who make significant efforts to address these topics, both in Bible studies *and* in sermons, do well to tap into the theological inquiries of these young adults. However, as modeled through Peter and Jesus, even when churches have sufficiently provided teachings that resonate with the young adults they seek to engage, there are still generational doubts that need to be addressed to prevent black Millennials from sinking away from the faith. Questions about the authority of Scripture, patriarchal practices, unprecedented access to information about other viable Afrocentric faith traditions, and the black church's response to (or refusal to engage) conversations around human sexuality seem to be four of the most prominent sources of doubt for black Millennials deciding whether or not to engage congregations on the waters of spiritual formation. In the following section, we will briefly examine each of these areas in turn.

Assumptions of Authority

At the heart of the worship experience at our church in Houston, Texas, is the dynamic preaching of our senior pastor, Dr. Marcus D. Cosby. Each week, people of all ages come to hear the Word of the Lord as preached through our pastor, and many respond to messages with great joy. One of the hallmarks of our pastor's teaching is its bibliocentric nature. When the sermon is reaching its apex, it is not uncommon to hear our pastor yell, "And the Biiiiiiiible says!" before quoting the text to support his point. The congregation most often responds favorably to this declaration, affirming their faith and trust in the truths that are being communicated from the Bible. But will this affirmation of the words of the Bible hold up among black Millennials?

Our study revealed that the Bible or sacred Scripture is still the primary source for black Millennials' spiritual formation. Black Millennials still esteem the Bible and utilize the Scriptures in conversation with their own personal experiences to shape their understandings about God and their place in the world. Yet nearly half of black Millennials we surveyed do not view the Bible as infallible and without error—a clear departure from the "if God said it, I believe and that settles it" mentality of previous generations. In many ways, the Scriptures are only as true to black Millennials as can be verified by their life experiences—not the other way around. With the widespread shifts in social and sexual norms that may not align with traditional interpretations of biblical texts, the proliferation of literature that raises suspicions about the process of biblical canonization, and the rise in popularity of atheist and other spiritual movements that question the integrity of the Scriptures, there is a growing consensus that humankind's hands have played a heavier role in the creation of both the Christian canon and the Christian church's doctrine than previously thought. To that end, some of the hardest work that churches seeking to disciple black Millennials will face is elevating and explaining the authority of Scripture.

In many ways, black Millennials have an innate hermeneutic of suspicion—and no text, tradition, or teaching is exempt from being questioned and critiqued. The freedom to question is a part of the wiring of this generation, sometimes called Generation "Y" (Why) not only because they follow Generation X but because they have been allowed and emboldened from childhood to express objection and dissension and to question the authorities in their lives in ways Baby Boomers never dared. Moreover, access to the Internet and other databases of knowledge only expand Millennials' opportunities to be exposed to diverse ways of thinking that support their assumptions, even when these assumptions do not line up with biblical teaching or church doctrine.

Therefore it is imperative, as mentioned in the previous chapter, for leaders to take seriously the task of investing in theological education. This does not simply mean going to the latest preaching conference or gatherings to exchange the latest "best practices" from leaders of growing congregations. This investment must be primarily theological. While a seminary education will not teach you everything about God or church history, a good seminary should help expose leaders to writers and resources that can help answer some of the questions about biblical authority. Good theological education can also help leaders be apologists for the Christian faith by making them aware of theologies and philosophies that young adults are being exposed to outside of the church.

Even beyond the willingness to invest in theological education, church leaders and clergy must also be well-read. Dr. James Henry Harris, Distinguished Professor and Chair of Homiletics and Practical Theology at the School of Theology at Virginia Union University, often reminds preachers to read, and read widely, as a spiritual discipline. It will not suffice to only know quotes from one's favorite Christian televangelist or dead apologist, but to read books and articles from opposing viewpoints, other religions, and other cultures to be more prepared for the queries of black Millennials wrestling with the authority of Scripture.

Patriarchy

One day after the inauguration of the forty-fifth president of the United States, a massive demonstration was held across the nation that would come to be known as the Women's March.

Millions of protesters organized and demonstrated around the world in support of women's rights and a host of other concerns (including healthcare, immigration reform, and LGBTQ rights) while simultaneously sending a message aimed squarely at President Trump. Following a campaign full of offensive rhetoric and behavior toward women, organizers sought to send a message that misogyny, sexism, and patriarchal systems would not be tolerated by this new wave of young leaders and activists. Among those crowds were tens of thousands of black Millennials, including many Millennials of faith, who demonstrated to show that they would not accept the denigration or devaluation of women in any space of engagement—not in their government and not in the house of God.

In a society where women are breaking through barriers and proverbial glass ceilings in education, the workforce, and even as presidential party nominees, congregations must take a hard look at the role of gender in their theology and in their ministry and leadership models. Our study suggests that black Millennials have very few hang-ups around the ability of women to lead, teach, preach, and pastor. But for many churches, these ideas are still a source of great tension.

In short, black Millennials have doubts about twenty-first-century churches who doubt the validity and call of women who work as leaders in every other space but the church. Much of this tension, as with issues of sexuality, are rooted in scriptural interpretations that have shaped church doctrine and tradition. In many cases, congregations who are viewed by Millennials as oppressive or "outdated" in this area are operating with the understanding that they are simply living by the Word of God without compromise in a godless society. As the church moves forward into future decades, we are challenged to continue to read widely—even in the biblical text itself—to reshape our understandings of God and gender roles in the church and society and to seek to embrace ethics of love and liberation.

VALUABLE VOICES

Featured Millennial: Rev. Neichelle R. Guidry, PhD, age 32, Founder of Shepreaches Solutions, Chicago, IL

Defining patriarchy . . .

The definition that I am trying to use as my running definition is actually Traci West's definition in her book *Wounds of The Spirit*.[1] She just has this really holistic definition that talks about patriarchy as the systematic and systemic devaluation of the worth and the value of women. . . . [P]atriarchy has constructed gender along a male-female binary that will always privilege men over women. What we see with patriarchy is, first of all, that it privileges the bodies, the perspectives, and the lives of men over women. But what it also does is create this gender binary that's really antiquated given the fact that gender is being discussed now along a spectrum of gender identity that is not conforming to this binary of male-female.

Patriarchy also has had a way of defining acceptable roles and behaviors for men and women. That's how you get to the idea of what is a man or what is a woman. A man is strong, a man is powerful, a man is at the head. A woman is submissive, a woman is kind, a woman is meek. We construct the gender idea off of biology and on the binary. It's already kind of set us up for a fascist situation that is dehumanizing for anyone who's not a white male. It's imperialist, it privileges the wealthy over the poor, and [it] has really stratified our community.

Patriarchy in the black church . . .

In the black church, it has really impacted everything from the leadership of the black church to the running definition of what it means to be a "good Christian man" or a "good Christian woman." On any given Sunday, you're likely to

walk into four out of five black churches and the face of
the leadership, the body of the leadership, is predominantly
male. Even if you were to have, say, a Trinity [United
Church] where all but one associate is a woman the senior
is still a male because of this kind of inundation—spiritual
inundation—of patriarchy. We always ascribe the head position to a man. When it comes down to how we're socialized
in the black church, particularly in regards to sexuality,
patriarchy has kind of defined two very different scripts. To
a man, you are not really socialized to be as sexually conservative as the women are, and you're definitely not demon-
ized for being sexual beings in the same way that women
are. You hear stories of a situation where a young woman
has gotten pregnant, as we like to say, "out of wedlock."
She thinks of all these consequences in her church community—[you] can't sing anymore, you got to sit down, you got
to make an explanation and an apology. But all the while,
what about the guy? How has he been held accountable for
his role in creating this human being?

Patriarchy has just made it very hard for women to really
flourish, not only as leaders, but also as humans. Now the
sad part about this is that it's not only men who kind of
enact and participate in patriarchy. Women do the same
thing. Sometimes we do it at an even greater rate. I have
many memories of women telling me I couldn't preach or
that I had to dress a certain way to preach or talk a certain
way to preach. I think we've all kind of been privy to the
recent example of Juanita Bynum's very patriarchal, very
misogynist rant on Facebook Live, basically condemning
black women for everything like wearing body-con dresses
to wearing lipstick. This kind of, like, hyper-policing. That's
from another woman! So I think it's very important as we
discuss patriarchy in the black church that men are not the
only components of it. Women are also preserving the legacy
and the role of patriarchy in the black church.

On textual tensions and interpretations . . .

One of the things we have to remember—and this is kind
of the tension with the text itself—is that, yes, it is God-
breathed, and yes, it is God-inspired—but it is a human
construction. It is a compilation that was done through
the ingenuity of human beings who had their own sets of
values and their own sets of perspectives. And if we're really
honest, most of them were men and they were patriarchal
men. Some would even be called misogynist men. We have
to just keep that in mind. I think that sometimes when we
think about the Bible as an ancient text one thing that we
don't think about is that everyone brings their own experience and insights to their interpretation of everything. Just
like the people who canonized the text had their values and
insights, we have our values and insights that really make up
our own hermeneutic today.

The second piece would be, we have some fine tuning that
we have to do on our biblical hermeneutic—how we read the
text, how we interpret it, how we apply it, how we preach it.
Again, I look to people like Renita Weems, Cain Hope Felder,
and Delores Williams who have shown us and given us ways
to bring wholeness to our humanity, to our interpretation
to the Bible. Some of us don't even realize that when we're
reading the Scripture in oppressive and old-school ways,
[that] we're employing white supremacist hermeneutics that
are actually working against us. I would just encourage us
to think very seriously and personally about what is shaping how we read the Bible. What is it that's influencing our
relationship with the Bible? Then possibly [consult] the work
of African American biblicists who have given us ways to
read the text from an African American perspective. I think
that when we read from that perspective, we start to see that
as long as we're oppressing women in our readings of Paul or
in our readings of Deuteronomy, we're also implicitly reading
ourselves back into enslavement.

Considerations for churches seeking to provide future formation for black Millennials . . .

I think as it relates to gender, as it relates to community, as it relates to activism—I think that the church could probably do really well to study the current movement for black lives. In all of those different organizational generations, whether in Black Lives Matter, the Black Youth Project, Campaign Zero—these are organizations that are really thinking through what it means to make change together, and really thinking through models of leadership that are non-hierarchical, that make space for people who have traditionally been on the margins to come into the center, and really kind of embodying collective leadership. This movement as a whole provides a really compelling conversation partner right now to churches who want to cultivate the future formation of Millennials primarily, because Millennials are at the helm of this movement right now. Rather than looking to a Millennial from within and kind of tokenizing them as the Millennial voice, the movement is really a paradigm of Millennial community, Millennial organizing, Millennial gender work that could be really beneficial to the church.

Alternative Religious Traditions

In 2011, I came across an informative article by Chika Oduah entitled, "Are blacks abandoning Christianity for African faiths?"[2] In it, Oduah observes African Americans who were raised in Christian homes but had since shifted to popular West African religions like the Ifa Yoruba spiritual tradition, Palo, Candomble, Umbanda, and Santeria. Oduah chronicles the frustrations of young people who had begun to doubt some of the teachings of the Christian tradition and the trustworthiness of Christian leaders, and were seeking spirituality that was more Afrocentric. My study suggests that black Millennials desire spiritual experiences and teaching where their blackness is reflected, and it is no surprise that African religious traditions are increasing in popularity among this generation. As this generation seeks to find their personal and collective identities, many are researching their ancestry and exploring the customs, languages, and spiritualties associated with their countries of origin. For them, the church does not have a monopoly on God, and as technology continues to make the global community smaller, black Millennials have all the access they need to explore African spiritual traditions.

While the church must be aware of this slow but significant shift toward other Afrocentric religious traditions, the truth is that many Millennials throw out *all* boxes as it relates to what they can and cannot believe. Rather than embracing all of the tenants of any particular religious tradition, we are in many ways living in the age of à la carte spirituality. Let the foodie in me try to explain.

When people go to a restaurant, the restaurant normally provides a menu with featured dishes combined in a certain way that cannot be changed. However, most restaurants also offer selections à la carte, or as separate items rather than as part of a set meal. This is the religious landscape and mindset for many black Millennials. If I look at a religious meal plan and do not like all of the ingredients of any one particular faith or practice, I can piece my spiritual meal together à la carte—taking the discipline of Islam, the love ethic of Christianity, the meditation practices of Hinduism, and so forth. While this may be an uncomfortable reality for many who have been steeped in the tradition of the church, it is normative for many black Millennials in search of the Divine.

VALUABLE VOICES

Featured Millennial: Empress Aset Sekhmet Maut, age 30,
Spiritual Advisor and Intuitive Healer, Ansonia, CT

On shifting away from the church . . .

I did grow up going to church. We went regularly, but we were not in the church every single Sunday. But we did get there. It was always a sense of community for me. It was always a place where I felt safe. It was always the place where I felt the Lord lives and you could go and see your family and your friends and all that kind of stuff. It was important to me, when I had kids, to make sure that my kids would find a place where their souls would be protected.

It was ultimately me doing a journey of self-discovery that changed my religious beliefs. When I started having kids and I was going all natural—trying to find myself— I started to question my beliefs. And so, I believe that it was [when I was reading] Ephesians 6:5 that says, "Slaves, obey thy earthly master, as you would me your God," and I was like, "That can't be right." I remember sitting there and thinking, "If my God is a jealous God and if he is omnipotent, he wouldn't tell me, a slave, to obey a man the same way that I would [God]." And so, that really got me searching for what I found to be other fallacies or inconsistencies in the Bible. And then I was like—it just made me really question to the point where I was finding the evidence against so much of it, that I could no longer believe it. And because of that, I started straying away from the church. I started to find myself, find the temple in myself, and move away from the church setting.

As far as other fallacies inside the Bible, I started looking into Kemetic spirituality and I was finding that a lot of [the Bible] was, what I thought at the time, just copying the original stories of the gods and the goddesses. Ra, Horus, Set, and all of those Egyptian gods and goddesses. And so, I was comparing the two and once I felt like it was a copycat, that's when I said, "I can't with this." I felt like it was an allegorical tale more than it was factual, as I used to feel it was in the past.

On her journey of self-discovery . . .

My journey of self-discovery, I would say, started almost four years ago. What I really believe started it was wanting to find out who I am. I suffered from anxiety, really bad anxiety. And it was always this feeling like there is something I'm supposed to be doing, but I don't know what it is I'm supposed to be doing. I also was living in what I called "the hamster-wheel cycle," where I would wake up, take care of my kids, go to work, cook and clean the house, put the kids to sleep, spend a couple of hours with my husband, go to bed, and do it again and again and again. And it was driving me crazy, and I kept telling myself, "There has to be more to life than this." And so it started about four years ago. I guess when I went natural. I just kept looking at the fact that I love this big hair. It kept calling me, like, "This is your hair, these are your roots. Find your roots." And then one day, I literally took scissors and went in the bathroom and cut off all of my relaxed hair. Which is crazy for me. And I just said, "Okay, well, you know this is me." Then after that I did [an] ancestry DNA test to find out where I came from. And again, this is just me trying to find out who I am and where I came from. And so I did that, I got the test, and they were pretty good but I still wanted to know more. I said, "I still feel like I can go deeper than this."

That's when I came across the ancient Egyptian spirituality. And that's also the period when I was having children and I wanted my kids to know where they were coming from. And so on February 22, 2016, I downloaded a book on my tablet about Egyptian spirituality at one o'clock in the morning. I started reading it and I couldn't stop reading it. And, without exaggeration, for two weeks straight there was this insatiable hunger for knowledge that I could not quench. I would literally wake up. I would drop one of the kids off at school. I would take my baby girl and put her in front of the TV and I would read, read, read, read, read, until it was time to feed her for lunch. I'd feed her, pay her a little bit of attention, put her back in front of the TV and read, read, read, until four o'clock in the morning. I'd go to sleep for two hours, wake up, and do it again. My ex-husband would say, "You can't keep doing this. Do you realize you are not sleeping and you're not eating?" And I was like, "I can't stop learning." It was the weirdest thing. I could not put this book down. And it wasn't just the book. There were multiple sources of information. It was the craziest thing.

I found later that there was a sense of the awakening process, and at the end of the two weeks, I was changed. I said, "Yeah, I see the world differently." I was like, "I have to find out where I came from. What's this religion I feel trapped in?" In terms of sexuality, they tell you no sex before marriage. That was something I was always worried about. They tell you if you get divorced, you'll burn in hell. They tell you all this kind of stuff. I felt I needed to question everything. It just told me to question everything. And from then, that's what I started doing.

I asked to be divinely guided. I said, "I'm going on this path and I feel lost." I went through a period of depression and anxiety. There were times where I wasn't eating for two or three days at a time. And I would just eat not to pass out. I was going through and I didn't want to do anything. I lost interest in my hobbies. I loved yoga and cooking [before] and I didn't want to do anything. I loved to do my hair [before] and I didn't want to do my hair. I didn't want to do anything. And it was because God was trying to wake me up, shake me and tell me, "You have a purpose, and you need to find it." I remember literally one day getting on my knees and surrendering, and saying, "God, use me as a conduit. Wherever you say, 'Go,' I'm going to go. Because the way I'm doing it, it's not working." I said, "Whatever it is that you need me to do, however it is that you need me to serve you, I'm ready and I'm willing to go." And then that's when stuff started changing.

That's when I started to find different things and new interests such as herbs and stuff. Like Shamanism, I came across articles about Shamanism. Or I'd hear a random radio commercial, "Oh this shamanist . . . " and I'd say, "Shamanism?" And I'd go home and I'd start researching that. I'd start learning about herbs and spices and how to make balms and salves and other things. Then one day I'm divinely guided toward Tarot cards. I'll go and find a few readers, and then the next day I'm in the shop and there are these Tarot cards in front of me and I get them. Then I'm divinely guided to do this, divinely guided to do that. So, right now I call myself an Omnist (if we have to put labels on it, because I really hate labels). I call myself an Omnist, which means that I take different parts of spiritualties and different religions and I create a spirituality that is custom to myself.

My friend said, "So you're just taking like the good parts of all the religions and using those?" And I said, "That's actually what I'm doing." Is that so wrong to do? Because again, while I do feel like the Bible is still riddled with fallacies and inconsistencies, I think there's some beautiful messages that I take from the Bible. There are still ways that I use the Bible even with my numerology and things. But I do not believe in the traditional sense, anymore, of heaven and hell. And I believe you create your heaven, and as an Omnist, this is how I look at life: I think that all paths lead to God. My theory is that you can see things in three ways: you can see them scientifically, you can see them religiously, or you can see them spiritually. But it's all the same thing. For instance, if you're a religious person, if you're a Christian, you're going to be talking about Adam and Eve. If you're a scientific person, you're going to be talking about atoms and electrons. If you're a spiritual person, you might go [to] Egyptian spirituality and talk about Asar and Aset. But it's all the same thing. It's just God.

You should know that there's a struggle involved in this journey, in this transition. Man cannot serve two gods. I always say to myself, "Man cannot serve two gods—faith or fear." This journey breaks you down. It's called the "dark soul of night." It's a journey, your spiritual awakening. It's your journey of your soul calling itself . . .

On the idea of being "spiritual but not religious . . ."

I say that same thing. Religion is Judaism, it is Christianity, it is Catholicism. Religions are structured systems. The systems are in place with rules and beliefs that those who subscribe to that system have to follow. You may not necessarily agree with it, everything, but they'll tell you, "You can't pick and choose." If you're Catholic—you got to go to Mass, you got to do this, duh-duh-duh-duh. If you're Christian, you have to tithe, you have to do this, you have to do that. That is a religion. Spirituality is more when you're connecting yourself to nature and the original way of life, if I had to define it. Spirituality is when you start to sync your body to the moon cycles, when you start to give praise to the food that you eat because you respect how long it took to grow. You have respect for animals and nature and God's creatures. It's when you become one with the world around you, when you know that you are part of this one, breathing, living organism. We are all one, God is in all of us, we are all in God. It's all connected. That's spirituality. There are no set rules. Nobody's going to tell you, "You say you are a pagan, so you can't do rituals on Saturday," or, "You say that you're Kemetic, so you can't . . . " There are practices within spirituality, but they are not as limited as religions are.

Final words to the church . . .

Change is not always seen as a good thing in these churches. If they are trying to garner and keep the interest of the young black youth, they're going to have to relate to the young black youth. Now we know they're shifting more towards spirituality. In respects to zodiac astrology, we left the Piscean age where you're talking about gurus and going outside of yourself for help. We're moving into the Aquarian era—when you are your own temple, you know what I'm saying? Your body is your own temple.

Teach people how to heal themselves. Do I think that people are going to, in a mass number, pray themselves up and start coming back to church because of it? No. But if your goal is to reach these people and get the Word to these people, then yes—have the sermons, but show them how to meditate at home. Show them how to create home altars. Also, be a little open-minded to the other—don't be so limited and exclusive and have so many restrictions, because young people don't appreciate working under boundaries.

Teach the youth. Teach them to meditate at home, teach them yoga. Integrate it into the church—crystals and all these kinds of things. Hopefully these things aren't too offensive, because I know that churches are very sensitive about things like this. Just nature and teaching them well-ness, teaching them mental health, teaching them how to do things when they're not inside of the church. You don't have to run to church and throw yourself on the altar when you need assistance. You can get on your knees and get immediate assistance! Teach them how to heal themselves from anywhere, and then they'll come back for that learning. Then you're also teaching them how to do it themselves in the real world, and I think that would bring more membership of the youth back.

Human Sexuality

The final doubts that must be addressed with black Millennials are birthed from the Christian church's traditional teachings and practices around human sexuality. While many black Millennials who grew up in the church have been exposed to teachings regarding sexual purity, chastity, and abstinence, there is an increasing number of black Millennials who love God but do not feel there is sufficient biblical or physiological support to back these teachings. Some black Millennials have dismissed the teachings of the church as sexually oppressive and obsolete—antiquated ideas for a time long gone by. Moreover, black Millennials who also identify as members of the LGBTQ community continue to walk away from congregations—not because they do not love Jesus, but because they do not feel safe in spaces where the entirety of their humanity is not affirmed. For many black Millennials who identify as queer, whom they love and the ways in which they express this love sexually are not sinful behaviors to be modified, but are God-given assets to their personhood. In recent years, more attention has been placed on ensuring protections and equity for the growing community of black transgendered men and women—some of whom are are being murdered or are becoming victims of suicide at alarming rates. The call to the Christian church is clear. These conversations about sexuality cannot be avoided, and serious theological, scientific, and emotional consideration and investment must be made as churches attempt to find their footing and articulate their stances in the twenty-first century.

VALUABLE VOICES

Featured Millennial: Rev. Verdell A. Wright, age 33, Licensed Clergy, PhD Student, Washington, DC

On the roles of LGBTQ allies at the intersection
of black faith . . .

In terms of sexuality and gender, what I would have to speak towards is more the allies, the people who say, "I'm on board. LGBTQ, whatever part of the alphabet, I'm with it," all of that. They need to actually do something besides talk and have panels. They need to be the ones to go and challenge the pastors, the preachers, whoever it is of the hour. I think that one reason why we have not moved further with this in the black church context is because our allies don't push.

Someone like me, there's little I can do. I'm on the fringes and the outskirts of the black church—even though I've been there, I was licensed there, all of that. I don't have the same level of power or access. But someone who says, "I am an ally. I am the cisgender person, I'm straight and I'm an ally," or whatever. You need to be the one to go and talk to your pastor when they screw up. You need to be the one, say, if there's a Men's Day and the man preaching says something homophobic or fem-bashing, you need to go say something, not just like my picture [on Facebook] when you see that I'm on a date, but [you] need to actually work to make this place safe. You have more access than I do, and I think that's something from what I've seen that has been sorely lacking, particularly in more black liberal circles. It's great you wrote a Facebook status and you may have written an article. That's very cute. Now what needs to happen is, when someone at your church does or says something, you need to come at them with the intensity and the ferocity that you expect everybody else to do for you. Which also means that in the same way someone wrote the article about women not being pastors and everybody made a hashtag and went bananas over it, that's how you need to be for queer people, except that you're not.

Finally, allies need to understand the various intersections. Queer people are everyone. Women, men, non-gender-conforming. Queerness is not . . . I think queerness encompasses so many people and groups that if it's not you dealing with this issue of queerness, know that queerness impacts so many people in a variety of ways. Maybe it's someone who never told you. Maybe it's the mother who has a queer child. It's also some things that this impacts. It's really a community issue and what I really would like to see—again, I'm not talking about those who do not affirm queerness, we know what they think—but the folks who consider themselves progressive or liberal have to do more than just like Facebook statuses and have nice conferences. It needs to be, start to challenge things on the ground zero where they are, so that way these places can be extra safe. It doesn't do me any good that you had a council, that you had a panel at [the Samuel DeWitt] Proctor [Conference], if it does not translate to somehow a church house being safer or being better. It has to be more than just, "Oh well, they said that," or it has to be more than just, "Oh well, he said be nice to everybody." That's too generic and we aren't that generic with other issues. That's what I will say.

On safe spaces for black Millennials who identify as LGBTQ . . .

I think, generally speaking, a safe space is a place where you can go where your whole humanity will be affirmed like everybody else's. I think that's where sometimes the break-down is. When you say, "Everybody is welcome," sure, I can come in and sit in the seat or even sing in the choir and give you money—but I won't be able to get married there, or you won't ordain me, or there's certain levels of participation in the church that I can't access simply because of queerness. That's not a safe space. And just because someone's not screaming, "Faggot, faggot," from the pulpit doesn't mean that this place is actually safe. I've experienced that. As a minister, I've been in pulpits where they made a joke insinuating that somebody is "funny" and I know these people were very nice. They'd never intentionally dog anybody out, but once that joke happened, it was within a month and a half I was gone and I was on the ordination track.

To know that your humanity is going to be affirmed, that you'll be allowed to participate in any area of the church, that your character is going to be the thing that is a requirement, not who you are, who you're in a relationship with, who you have sex with, who you love—all those types of things, how you present those things, [is] going to make a difference. To me, that's what a safe space is. I think other people will have different views, but for me, I think that needs to be the base level. Open and affirming means that when you have Men's Day, it's not "Straight, He-man Pastor Day," [but] that a trans woman can come and preach at your church. I know this is probably asking for a lot, I understand, but that's what safety looks like. Having gender-inclusive bathrooms. We always talk about the building fund, but can we have one of those?

Again, these things can't all appear overnight. I get that, and I want to say something about that critique, too. I get that oftentimes people say, "Well, things take time." I want to say to that, "Duh!" Nothing happens instantaneously, but I also want to challenge the idea that this thing will take longer than it needs to. It's only taking so long because we as a group don't want to move. That's what's taking so long. We can do this if we actually commit to it. We can make some change. We can actually do this and I think that is the thing when it comes to the safe space. It's like, "Oh, we need time." How much more time do you need to discuss not being cruel and affirming people? The process takes time, but we aren't even really engaging the process. I don't think we're honest about that, but that is what a safe space is for me. I think just generally speaking, just a place where, you know, where you are safe from attack, where you are safe from harm, where you're not going to be made the butt of every problem and joke in the black community. Where your mental health is not going to be attacked. You're not going to be literally and figuratively spoken to death about who you are or yourself or any experience that you may have had or [are] having. That's a safe space. Safe means that I'm able to do what everybody else does in the church, regardless of my sexual orientation. Regardless of my gender identity, I can be and exist the way everybody else does in that space.

On resources and "next steps" for congregations in conversation with black LGBTQ Millennials . . .

They have to pick up *Sexuality and the Black Church*[3] by Kelly Brown Douglas because she talks about why this conversation around sexuality and gender is so difficult for black people, particularly black Christian people, and she does a good [job] of discussing that and putting those issues in context. That way, we understand why we talk about things the way that we do and [she gives] us tips to come out of that. That's a good place to start. Another book that I would [recommend] is *Our Lives Matter* by Pamela R. Lightsey.[4] She is giving another womanist account . . . she's talking as a queer woman herself and just talking about why this matters. I think she gives a good first-person account, if you will, of why that makes a difference. I would recommend those two books. Instead of a third book, I'm going to recommend a resource, ManyVoices.org. It's a black church movement that works to talk about the issues around sexuality and gender.

> That's a good place to start, a good place to reach out to, a good place to build information. They have informational packets and things like that. It's stuff that you can pick up and read. If you don't want to read those first two books, that's a good place to start. I would start there.

Those Who Were in the Boat: Navigating the Noise

After Jesus invites Peter to communicate the source of his doubts, they walk back toward the boat full of disciples. The text does not give us much of the dialogue from the boat throughout the ordeal, but we can imagine that from the time the disciples initially see the "ghost" on the lake to the time that the boat gets back to shore, the boat is noisy! As Peter is contemplating whether or not to get out of the boat, we can hear the disciples telling him that he is crazy, that he can't walk out on the water, that what Peter is seeing is not the divine being that he thinks it is. Peter has to find a way to navigate the noise from his brothers in the boat in order to get the nerve to walk out on the lake and engage with Christ. After witnessing that encounter, the other disciples begin to ask questions about the experience, to affirm Jesus, and to inquire about engaging in the phenomenal with Jesus as well.

Like Peter, black Millennials are growing up in a noisy world! Each day they must discern the difference between real news and "fake news," reality and alternative facts. Technology has provided black Millennials with access to various faiths, religions, practices, and spiritualities—many boasting claims to the truth. Media continues to portray the black church with damning stereotypes, while black Millennial Christians are in many cases being forced to operate as unprepared apologists in a post-Christian society. It's a noisy time—but the Body of Christ must be prepared to help black Millennials navigate the noise of the boats they're in, having answers to the doubts of the Peters we seek to engage, so that ultimately young disciples will be able to walk with Christ without sinking in the midst of the stormy seas of life.

Walking on Water

1. What are some of the questions about the Bible and church history that *you* have? Where can you go to get solid answers on them?

2. Can you identify patriarchal practices or systems in your congregation or ministry? What steps can be taken to address these issues?

3. Does your church leadership have any knowledge of West African spirituality? How does your ministry communicate the Afrocentricity of the biblical text?

4. Where does your church stand on LGBTQ issues? Marriage? Ministry leadership? How are these views communicated to the congregation? How do they line up with Rev. Verdell Wright's definition of "safe space"?

Notes

1. Traci West, *Wounds of The Spirit* (New York: New York University Press, 1999).

2. Chika Oduah, "Are blacks abandoning Christianity for African faiths?" October 19, 2011, http://thegrio.com/2011/10/19/african-religions-gain-following-among-black-christians/.

3. Kelly Brown Douglas, *Sexuality and the Black Church: A Womanist Perspective* (New York: Orbis Books, 1999).

4. Pamela R. Lightsey, *Our Lives Matter: A Womanist Queer Theology* (Oregon: Pickwick Publications, 2014).

CHAPTER EIGHT

Gennesaret

"When they had crossed over, they landed at Gennesaret."

MATTHEW 14:34

Peter and Jesus' experience on the lake is an incredible miracle, one that sends shock waves throughout the boat as they return to the disciples. Variations on the phrase "I still can't believe what we just saw!" can be heard throughout the boat, and with each passing minute, an appreciation for the power and person of Jesus grows within the men of the boat. Men who were once spectators as Jesus worked a miracle and exposed new possibilities to their friend Peter now are inquiring of Jesus for themselves as they row toward their destination. Caught up in the excitement of the moment and looking forward to more revelation, the disciple responsible for navigating the course of the boat calls to Jesus and asks, "Master, where to next? Where should we land?" Jesus briefly looks at Peter—still sitting in amazement at all that he has just experienced—and tells the disciple, "Gennesaret. We anchor in Gennesaret!"

Let me be transparent: as a "church baby," I have likely heard this story taught and preached hundreds if not thousands of times (ok, that might be a *slight* exaggeration). In most of the teachings on the text, the focus is on the drama that unfolds on the lake—concluding with Peter and Jesus returning to the boat where the disciples now have a new revelation of who Jesus is.

However, the back end of the text has significance as well. After a life-changing, divinity-revealing experience for Peter, it is no accident that the Gospel writer mentions where the disciples go next to be anchored. They land in the region of Gennesaret, a land that historians suggest was known for its lush vegetation, beauty, and fertility. It was called the "Paradise (or Garden) of Galilee" because of all the things that could be grown there. It is significant that after a life-altering encounter with Christ, Peter and the disciples would immediately land and be anchored in a place known for continuous growth!

Matthew 14:34 makes the call clear for congregations seeking to engage and disciple black Millennials in the twenty-first century. After these young adults take the risk of leaving their boats, engage the Divine on the water, and have a life-altering experience with Christ, it is important to ensure that we immediately connect them to programming, teaching, and discipleship opportunities that foster their growth! To be sure, many congregations and leaders assume that their methodologies, classes, and leaders are sufficient to facilitate spiritual growth among this generation. However, the black Millennials in my study suggested at least four key areas that congregations must consider to ensure that we are creating "Gennesarets" for them. Ultimately, creating Gennesarets for the Peters of this generation will require being intentional about our content, conductors, communities, and cocreators and co-laborers.

Content

As congregations consider the programming and teaching efforts geared toward the spiritual formation of black Millennials, a few considerations must be made with regards to the content that we provide. At the top of the list is relatability! Black Millennials report experiencing spiritual growth through the church when they are exposed to biblical teaching and preaching that relates to their life experiences. Black Millennials are less interested in "abstract" discussions about how many angels can fit on the head of a pin than they are in how the Bible speaks to the realities of student loan debt, relational drama, joining a sorority or fraternity in college, and helping them find purpose in this life. While black Millennials seem to crave a more topical approach to study, this is not to say black Millennials are disinterested in studying whole books of the Bible or obscure texts in the lectionary. However, it is the responsibility of the teacher to stress the application of the Scripture and the relevance of this text to the day-to-day realities these young adults face. Questions like "What would this look like today?" and "What does this text have to do with us?" must be answered for black Millennials in each session.

Content must not simply be relatable and intentionally applicable to the everyday lives of black Millennials, but must also be available in ways that are natural for the generation. My study suggests that young adults are not disinterested in spiritual edification and exploration, but are most often hindered by the availability of the material. In my study, black Millennials who regularly participated in the church acknowledged the value of teaching ministry offerings such as Sunday school, Bible study, and discipleship training courses, but they are often absent because of the day of the week or the time of day these offerings are held. It is imperative for churches to consider making content available in ways that are native to the black Millennial experience. Respondents suggested implementing online classes, videos, live streams, and social media to ensure that this desired content can be accessed at times that are convenient for the participant.

Additionally, the content must be presented in a way that honors the primary learning style of black Millennials. Ninety percent of black Millennials identify as visual or movement/hands-on learners, so the content of our Christian education materials must be presented via a multi-sensory experience. Multimedia presentations through software like Prezi and Microsoft Power-Point are almost a base-level requirement for teaching sessions with a generation whose lives revolve around screens and digital images. Also helpful are interactive ice breakers and group activities that illustrate the main ideas of the lesson while providing students with the opportunity to move around and engage the subject matter among peers.

Conductors

My study revealed that the personality of the leader or teacher is paramount to increasing the willingness of black Millennials to engage the teaching ministries of our churches. Thankfully, some of the unwritten requirements for would-be teachers in previous generations do not hold weight among the majority of these young adults. The age of the teacher or leader is not a major issue for black Millennials. Though the primary preference identified in our study was a teacher or leader who was a few years older than them, the knowledge and competency of the teacher is a much more important factor. Black Millennials are not as concerned as previous generations with the gender of the teacher, and they affirm the ability of women to teach, preach, and lead in spaces of spiritual formation. In fact, in our study the vast majority of respondents indicated that they do not have a preferred gender for their Christian educators, but they do seek an educated teacher who is both knowledgeable and relatable. As stated in previous chapters, it benefits leaders and teachers to be well-educated on their topic of instruction to be able to anticipate and adequately answer the questions that these young adults have. "Relatability" in our study was defined as the ability to break down the truths and themes of the text and apply them specifically to the life circumstances of the waiting congregant. Black Millennials seek spaces where the Word is being taught and explained in a clear and engaging way by a welcoming and non-judgmental personality.

As previously stated, black Millennials indicate experiencing the most growth in spaces where the leader employs a teacher-as-facilitator model. This means that the pastor, teacher, or leader is primarily a facilitator of conversation around the topic and promotes open discussion and dialogue among the group. This facilitator should be well-versed in the topic and text that is chosen and should also have main ideas to impart. However, this model pushes the teacher not to operate primarily as an authoritative lecturer but as a facilitator of conversation who leads the group to come to various conclusions for themselves. These leaders have the boldness to correct when necessary but the patience to allow these young adults to wrestle (even out loud) long enough for the "lightbulb" to come on.

Community

Black Millennials value the opportunity to engage in the process of discipleship within a community of learners. As we conclude our college Bible study each Thursday night, I ask the students to circle up and we pause to acknowledge the first-time guests and the students who invited them. After greeting all of the first-timers, I always identify the students who participate in our Bible study as a family. In a society of familial diversity, fractured families, and individualistic paths to "success," it is meaningful for those young adults to feel connected to a tribe and to a group of peers who can help them grow. Again, in this model the "teacher" is not a lecturer but primarily a skilled facilitator of conversation within a group or community of fellow learners. The leader is educated and prepared to provide important insights about the text as needed but is also open to hear and learn from the input of the group. This community is best received when black Millennials are studying among peers of a similar age with common experiences. Black Millennials also value the ability to have open dialogue among peers, though the facilitator must ensure that dialogue does not lead the discussion too far away from the topic or lengthen the time of study too severely.

As we held focus groups and interviewed young adults for our study, one of the recurring themes that came up was intimacy. Several of the students who attend our college Bible study expressed a fear that our Bible study group would become too big and lose its family feel. In fact, some visited the larger young adult programming and were overwhelmed by the huge mass of people—feeling like they in some way lost their voice in the conversation as well as their connectivity to others. I see this revelation as a challenge and tremendous opportunity for congregations. It suggests that, while a ministry does not need to be gigantic to be effective (though Millennials need to see themselves reflected in the congregation), they do need to feel connected in an intimate way to stay engaged. Small-group ministry models for study and fellowship seem to be effective tools for congregations seeking to build Gennesarets for the Peters of this age.

Cocreators and Co-laborers

One of the tragic mistakes of many twenty-first-century congregations is to assume we know what will attract and ultimately help black Millennials to grow without ever making space to be in conversation with them. My doctoral research was greatly impacted by the work of Jeff Fromm and Christie Garton. In their book *Marketing to Millennials: Reach the Largest and Most Influential Generation of Consumers Ever,*[1] Fromm and Garton utilize their combined expertise as marketers and social entrepreneurs to present a guide for effectively marketing to the Millennial generation. The book was birthed out of their comprehensive research study on Millennials in the U.S. entitled "American Millennials: Deciphering the Enigma Generation." The authors analyze their research findings and present guiding principles and trends. This book was helpful to my research by first highlighting distinctive qualities of the Millennial generation and providing insights on how organizations can help their messages be heard in a noisy world. The authors' conversation around the principle of Millennials as cocreators—participants in the creation and promotion of products—provides invaluable insight for congregations seeking to connect and engage black Millennials in spiritual development. In short, businesses and organizations who have been successful in gaining the attention and investment of Millennials have all given them opportunities to help create and provide directional input in the development of the products and services that they will ultimately consume. From deciding the new flavor of potato chips that a company will release to voting on which artists will perform at popular award shows, it has become normative for black Millennials to be given a say in what they will consume and participate in.

The church should take note of this reality and find ways to hear the voices of the Peters that they seek to engage—asking, for example, to identify the areas of study or social justice causes that are most important to them. Congregations can poll this target audience to help develop curriculum and teaching series around the topics that matter most to the young people in that context. Having a voice in the direction of the teaching and spiritual formation process only increases the desire for a young adult to invest in the congregation and to invite others to participate. As cocreators, black Millennials are also empowered when they are given the tools to study and develop on their own. While the teacher-as-authority model of previous generations has been sufficient for some, the access to information that black Millennials have today makes it necessary to give them tools to study texts and exegete truth wherever they are—both inside and outside of the church sanctuary.

Finally, as stated in previous chapters, the goal must be to help these cocreators become co-laborers. Millennials do not simply want a seat at the table to discuss the direction of their spiritual formation; they want to be active leaders and workers in the ministries that service them. Congregations must think through ways to match the gifts and talents of those they seek to serve with the needs of the church. To be sure, this does not mean simply throwing these Millennials onto volunteer teams to serve with the children and youth ministries. This means getting to know them well enough to properly place a young CEO or accountant on the church's trustee board or budgeting committee. As the young adults of this generation get opportunities to utilize their gifts and talents in the churches that they dare to engage on the waters, those congregations will become Gennesarets for young leaders growing in faith, love, and service to God and humankind.

VALUABLE VOICES

Featured Millennial: Rev. Chelir Grady, age 30, Campus Minister at Texas Southern University Intervarsity Christian Fellowship, Houston, TX

On one example of a ministry that has stimulated the growth of many of her black Millennial college students . . .

Have you heard of Hope City? It's one of the fastest-growing churches in Houston. Literally this church has been around for one year. It meets at Memorial High School and it has no intention of ever building a church building. It has moved from two services when it started in January of 2016 to six services: four services on Sunday and two services on Saturday night. In one year, with no church [building], and when I tell you people are getting *saved*—and there's no procedure. It's just, "You want to come to Christ, okay, we're going to be baptizing today. Get your shirt and let's go." They have shirts already ready for you. "Change your clothes and go." People love the service because [the pastor's] relatable and he talks about stuff that is not touched in most churches. [There are] people there that were going to my church. I have friends that were going to my church that have left and are now at Hope City. No, it's not even that they're at Hope City, they're actually *serving* at Hope City. They're on the usher board, they're the greeters. They go to the small group Bible studies that they have all throughout the city . . .

Everything's on social media. All of the stuff on social media has been related to movies, because [the pastor's] teaching a series utilizing movies to spark the sermonic conversation—and people are learning to adapt. I don't have to go to a church building. Just give me a space where I can come and talk about Jesus. I'll be good. Tell me how to understand and navigate the craziness of life. It's not about the time. If it's right, people are going to come to it. You just need the right people to be exposed. For example, I was going and I told all my friends, so now my friends are going. A lot of my friends that would come to that Saturday night service—they weren't going to anyone else's church. But when they heard [the pastor] had a church, they said, "Oh yeah, we're going there." You know? It's because the stuff that he talks about is relatable.

On how she has experienced growth in her campus ministry work . . .

One factor was empowering others and not putting everything on myself. Realizing and recognizing that God did not only gift you and that God has placed gifts and purpose in every part of the Body. Every member of the Body has a role. That's a big thing. Also recognizing when there's an issue and not sitting on those issues. I remember [in] the first two weeks of school saying, "Okay, guys, nobody is showing up." We could have just said, "All right, let's pray about it and hope." No, let's figure out what the issue is! That's my engineering background, knowing that if we continue the way we are right now, there's not going to be an Intervarsity at the end of this year. That was the case a lot of times. The first year we had 15 students or so by the end of that spring semester. Only, like, four of them returned. What do we do? I recognized, "Okay, at this point everybody's a part of Intervarsity because they love Chelir." I want them to be a part of Intervarsity because they love the Bible and they love Jesus. All we did since that first semester is just pour it into the students that we had, and we just studied the Bible and some Scripture and prayer. That's all we did. That's all we still do now, that's at the root and the foundation of everything we're doing. Understanding and making sure that whatever you're building, it has a solid foundation.

Then the intimacy thing, because one of my students was saying that we can't allow ourselves to become so structured that there's no fluidity. One of the girls said to some of her

> friends who do not attend the Intervarsity small groups, "Y'all go to Bible study on Monday nights, so obviously [your concern is] not that we're talking about Bible stuff." They replied, "Yeah, but it needs to be relevant, and also it's just more intimate. It's not so structured." That helps too.

Walking on Water

1. How would you assess the relatability of the content your ministry provides? How does it connect to the contemporary society and life-stage issues that black Millennials face?

2. What is the consensus about the personality and relatability of your primary teachers? What do they do well in terms of connecting to Millennials in the congregation? How might they improve?

3. What small-group spaces currently exist for young adults to fellowship and learn together? If none exist, how can you imagine creating these spaces in the next church year?

4. How do you currently make space for black Millennials to be cocreators and co-laborers in the spiritual formation activities of your ministry? What are new ways to empower them to lead in your ministry context?

Notes

1. Jeff Fromm and Christie Garton, *Marketing to Millennials: Reach the Largest and Most Influential Generation of Consumers Ever* (New York: AMACOM, 2013).

CHAPTER NINE

The More Things Change

"From the tribe of Issachar, there were 200 leaders of the tribe with their relatives. All these men understood the signs of the times and knew the best course for Israel to take."

1 CHRONICLES 12:32, NLT

As a child growing up at Rising Sun Baptist Church in Washington, DC, one of the hymns I frequently sang was "Hold to God's Unchanging Hand."[1] It quickly became one of my favorite songs, and the older I get, the more I appreciate the truth in the lyrics. The song opens with talking about God's relationship with time: while time brings "swift transition," we can place our hope in the unchanging and eternal nature of God. Those lyrics have always reminded me that God is the stabilizing force in an ever-changing society—and I've found great comfort in the idea that there are some truths and values we can rely on no matter where societal shifts take us.

I recognize that for many congregations and the people who lead them, the times that we live in can be strange and scary. Some fear an inability to keep up with every "swift transition" that accompanies this new generation. The social media fads seemingly come and go too quickly to master any one platform, and the technological advances that drive the way we engage in ministry and in the marketplace can feel invasive and too complex to keep up with. With the massive amount of information available to everyday consumers, young adults are constantly exploring and studying new ideas, philosophies, and religious beliefs that previous generations of the black church did not have to "compete" with or engage. The continuous flow of new scientific and archaeological discoveries in this millennium is challenging the way we understand the intersection of science and spirituality and will force churches to have tough conversations around evolution, space, and our Creation literature. Womanist and Queer theology continue to draw the support of black Millennials both in the academia and pews, and are serving to reignite theological conversations around issues of gender, sexuality, and equity in Christ.

Time is indeed filled with swift transition, and these transitions can be intimidating for congregations who seek to engage in transformative spiritual formation with black Millennials but do not feel prepared to transition with the times. As I have consulted and conversed with pastors and church leaders around Millennial engagement, many express a willingness to embrace change but a lack of resources to do so. With most churches in the U.S. having fewer than 100 members,[2] many congregations simply do not have the finances to invest in the technological upgrades needed to best engage these digital natives. Moreover, many congregations in search of more young adults do not currently have enough young adults to attract others to join a group of like-minded peers. With these realities in mind, many church leaders have valid questions about their ability to engage this emerging generation of church leaders, and ultimately about their ability to "survive the shift."

Do not be discouraged! Here's the good news: my study suggests that the more things change, the more things stay the same! It is likely that your church is already doing some of the things that will optimize the spiritual formation process for black Millennials. Based on the findings of my study, here are five strategies that any church can implement today that have proven to be effective in engaging black Millennials to grow with a particular congregation of ministry.

Genuine Community

As previously mentioned in this work, Millennials are a hyper-relationally driven generation. The importance of building genuine and loving communities cannot be overstated. In an age of Facebook facades and fickle friendships, it is refreshing for Millennials to find church communities where they are accepted and cared for. Remember, one of the fears of black Millennials who engaged in interactive Christian education experiences was the loss of intimacy, so smaller congregations have an opportunity to provide this level of intimacy and personalized care in a way that large congregations may struggle to achieve. Leaders can take time to know these young people by name and learn about their lives and backgrounds. Congregations may consider organizing small tribes or groups of young adults based on birthdays or zip codes and assigning young leaders to facilitate fellowship and study opportunities among the group. Create opportunities for seasoned professionals in the congregation to be matched and become mentors for Millennials in the congregation with similar interests. Ensure that greeters and ushers are hospitable and warm from the first meeting on the parking lot, and find ways to foster a family atmosphere within the congregation. In the event that your congregation does not have a significant number of young adults, collaborate and fellowship with other congregations to strengthen the level of programming provided. All of these things come without a price tag but go a long way toward creating safe space for black Millennials to engage in spiritual formation.

Community Engagement

The black church has always served as a pseudo–social service agency for the community, ensuring that families have what they need to survive and thrive. Churches seeking to engage black

Millennials must continue in this tradition of being the charitable hand and prophetic voice in the communities they serve. Many churches, large and small, are already doing the work! Some are providing soup kitchens and food pantries to provide hot meals and canned goods to those in need throughout the week. Others are housing clothing closets where members donate new and gently used garments that can be given to members of the local community who need clothes and shoes. Still others are maximizing the intellectual capital that exists within their congregation—proving tutoring services, English/Spanish language classes, pro-bono legal services, and more. It is not important for congregations to do *everything* in the community, but it is important that congregations are engaged in *something* that makes a visible and tangible difference for others. Millennials are world-changers and are wired to expect immediate gratification. Churches must provide opportunities for black Millennials to get their hands dirty and serve where they can immediately sense the impact of their work. Moreover, as previously discussed, it is not enough for churches to simply do the work. They must tell these stories so that young people are aware and energized about the work of their church.

Evangelism and Promotion

The principles of effective evangelism are ever-changing, and I would suggest that they are very different from the days of my childhood. When I was a child, Christians were encouraged to spread the gospel and the word about our local congregation by going door to door in the neighborhood—talking about Jesus and talking about the work of our churches. These days, door-to-door community canvassing has been abandoned by many churches in favor of the relational evangelism approach. Along with shifts in the ways that congregations spread the word about Christ are shifts in the way congregations spread the word about our local churches. In some cases, television, radio, and newspaper advertisements have given way to websites and social media campaigns. To be sure, churches must invest in quality websites and online giving opportunities, but how else might churches effectively compel Millennials to come to our local churches?

Believe it or not, my study revealed that the most effective way for congregations to promote their programming is not through social media or any media at all. Overwhelmingly black Millennials suggest that the most effective way to pull them in is through the personal invitation of another! In consumer-marketing terms, nothing is more effective at driving traffic than a brand ambassador—who has actually engaged with and been transformed by the brand—going back to her peer group to relay the message. In biblical terms, nothing is more effective at helping black Millennials grasp a true understanding of the power and person of Christ than a Peter who has a life-changing experience on the water with Jesus in view of his peers in the boat. Young people who are transformed and grow as a result of engaging our ministries become the best advocates and evangelists for us. They go back and compel friends, classmates, and coworkers to join them on the water and walk into new possibilities that they have experienced firsthand.

I need to stop here for a second to convey an important truth of the text that has meaning for our conversation. Though the text does not explicitly tell us how many disciples were in the boat with Jesus, we can assume that there are at least twelve of them (including Peter) making the journey. When Jesus gives the command to "come," the Greek tense used is plural, suggesting that Jesus invites *all* of the disciples to come to him on the lake. Yet of the twelve who are invited, there is only one who dares to engage the ghost on the water. This is important, because the same may be true for our congregations. In reality, we may only see a fraction of the Millennial population that we desire to engage actually walk through our church doors. However, if we can be faithful to opening the eyes and expanding the faith of the Peters who *do* come, those Peters can then go back to their respective boats and transform the lives of their peers. This method does not ensure that the work of our congregations will always get the numbers we desire or the credit for our efforts, but ultimately God will get the glory!

Effective Christian Education

Each Thursday evening at our college ministry Bible study, we begin our time together by having a student pray for us, by reading our memory Scripture together, and by reciting the books of the Bible together. One Thursday as we were reciting the books of the Bible, a strange feeling came over me. Standing in front of a room of black Millennials and listening to them recite the books of the Bible together, I had a strange revelation—*I'm becoming my dad*. Throughout my childhood, my father taught Bible study at our home church each Thursday night and would always begin the lesson with prayer, Scripture of the month (our memory Scripture), and the recitation of the books of the Bible. As a child, I did not have the books listed on a fancy LCD screen like I do for the young adults who attend our Bible study each week, but the sound was the same and the strategy was the same. The same way that I learned the books of the Bible, through weekly repetition, is the same way I am teaching our Millennial students the books of the Bible today. The same way I was able to internalize important Scriptures that I would need throughout my life is the same way I help our students internalize the Scriptures. The same open discussion format that my father has used for years so that Bible study attendees could talk through the Scriptures together is the same format that is best received by the Millennials I serve today. The more things change, the more things stay the same!

In previous chapters I paraphrased an axiom that I live by in ministry: as we continue to experience shifts in our society and culture, the message of the cross does not have to change but our methods must change. (Granted, some may suggest that many black churches need to rethink some of our theological positions.) In general, as it relates to our technology use, evangelism strategies, and use of space, I would apply this axiom. However, as illustrated in the work of the church of my youth, many of the strategies utilized to disciple me as a child are still useful tools for churches. As you consider some of the information in this book and some of the perspectives offered by the Valuable Voices included in this work, you may find that many of our Christian education tactics are effective. Be strong enough to ask questions of the young people you seek to serve to see what works for them—celebrating the tools already used by your ministry that work while being unafraid to abandon those that do not. In the end, the goal is not to hold on to our cherished Sunday school or discipleship models for nostalgia's sake, but to seek effective educational models that benefit the Peters who are willing to engage us on the water.

The Word Still Works

"You're going to do *what*?!"

I'll never forget the Sunday in 2017 when I went into the pastor's study to greet our associate pastor, Rev. Alexander E.M. Johnson, who was preaching that particular Sunday because our senior pastor was out of town. I asked if he needed anything, to which he replied, "Prayer, Reverend. I'm preaching in first-person." He said it so quietly that it didn't initially register what he was telling me he was about to do. In a church used to hearing the senior pastor stand week after week behind the pulpit, powerfully preaching in a contemporary version of the black Baptist preaching tradition, our associate pastor's decision to preach a narrative sermon from the perspective of a character in the Scripture was a clear departure from our normal pattern. The more I thought about it, the more nervous for him I became, unsure of how it would be received by the waiting congregation. When I asked why he chose to utilize that method, his answer was simply, "The Lord told me to." That was the end of our conversation.

What I soon discovered was that this first-person sermon was a masterpiece. At our first service, I stood at the conclusion of the message in tears—deeply moved by the clarity and content of the Word. Little did I know that just hours later at our 11:00 a.m. service, over 70 black Millennials would walk the aisles to join our church. We all stood in a mixture of amazement, humility, and gratitude as what seemed like an ocean of Millennials continued to respond to the Word and the call to join the Lord's church. What was more significant was that this occurred on a Sunday when our senior pastor was away, when the sermon was presented in a fashion that was out of the norm for us, and when worship was led primarily by a group of young adults who mirrored those who would join the church that day. Following the invitation to discipleship, I walked over to our associate pastor in tears and simply said, "Thank you for your obedience." What I witnessed that morning was an affront to the reports that black Millennials are disinterested in God and in God's church. It was a reminder that—when presented in a way that is authentic, compelling, relevant, and clear—the preaching of the Word of God still works!

My final encouragement to every teacher, preacher, or pastor who is reading this book and seeking to engage black Millennials in their spiritual formation process is this: continue to preach and teach the Word. As the writer of the hymn "Lift Him Up"[3] suggests, black Millennials have an appetite for the Bread of Life and it is up to us to keep lifting the name of Jesus high! Men and women of God, keep preaching the gospel! Keep lifting Jesus up, and God will continue to draw men and women to God's self and to God's church. Now go, have the tough conversations, make the appropriate investments, create the necessary safe spaces, and bid them to come!

VALUABLE VOICES

Featured Millennial: Rev. Candace Simpson, age 26, Educator, New York, NY

Important issues for Millennials that the Christian church must consider . . .

I think there are a lot of issues that are of importance to me and other Millennials. I think if we want anyone to believe what we say about this Christ that we follow, we now have to behave a lot differently. For example, I don't mean to say that one life is more important than another, but I do believe that's how we behave. In 2016, we had the murder of Alton Sterling, Philando Castile, and other black men at the hands of law enforcement, and it activated and galvanized our church communities because, of course, we're activated and galvanized by the very real threat against black men. 2017 proved to be such a deadly year for black transwomen and we did not address it the same way. Yet all these things are connected and require our attention. There's homophobia, transphobia, hyper-masculinity, gender binary—all these things contribute to the astronomical weight on transwomen who are not just being killed, but also can't find sustainable work. That's a problem, and just because we don't think we see black transwomen in our churches doesn't mean that is not also an issue. That's an issue, climate change is an issue, the school-to-prison pipeline is an issue, student debt is an issue, patriarchy is an issue. All you have to do is open the newspaper or even your news feed for 50 seconds and you will see that there are issues that exist in the real world beyond "Why don't people go to church?"

For example, a young person who is very close to me was pushed out of her home because of gentrification and landlords who were not honest or decent. And as I sit at these conferences, I'm asking, "What shall we say to these things? What are we saying about families that get displaced because of deportation, or families that get displaced because of gentrification, or their buildings are being torn down to put up a new gym? What are we going to say to these times?"

Final considerations for the Christian church . . .

I think we are going to have to wean ourselves from this need that we have to be all things to all people, and I think we're going to have to figure out the one, two, or even three things that we do well, and do that. We don't have to have an answer to every social issue, but I think we do have to make a claim about what it is that we're committed to, and then really organize deeply around those issues. For example, what would it look like for a church to be spiritually committed to dismantling the system of mass incarceration? A church that does everything from hiring formerly incarcerated persons and offering job training to having a group of people who just go to visit people in prison or write letters. What does it look like to deploy people to do that kind of work, because I think once you choose something to address, you will get people who are of all ages, all backgrounds, and all desires who want to plug in.

It just seems very simple to me that people want to be where they have a place to be, which means more than, like, Young Adult Sunday or youth retreats as our engagement. Those things are important and we should continue to do those things, but what is our sustained commitment to being a church and being followers of Christ with integrity? One of our [generational] values is authenticity, so if we find that we are at a church that doesn't feel authentic to us, that's a problem. It's a problem for the people who leave and it is a problem for the people who stay behind. Why would you want to be a part of an inauthentic church? How do we get around that?

As Millennials, we have to be careful that we don't get too self-righteous and too indignant. Youth is not forever, so we also [need to] ensure we make a claim, that we define what is important to us and how we behave as followers of Christ. Twenty years from now we will [still] be Millennials, but we will [no longer] be 20 to 37 years old. So we have to look [at] what habits we're cultivating now. We need to learn from the mistakes of previous generations, and that means we have to have relationships with each other that are meaningful and they're two-sided. We should feel that we can talk to people and they can talk with us, that we can offer critique and they can offer critique to us. Otherwise, like I said, we're going to be exactly where we've always been, and my kids' generation is going to say, "Mom, what happened to your generation?" I'll have to say, "Girl, I don't know!"

In the midst of it all, I'm trying to follow Jesus. To be honest, I really think all the other stuff will fall in line if we follow Jesus. It can't go wrong when you follow Christ. We have to be more committed to Christ than we are to the church, and that means sometimes we're going to have to follow Christ in the streets or to our local elected officials or to people who need advocates or what have you, but I think a lot of this conversation about generation really gets lost. We're losing why we even gather. We're here to do the work of justice and to lift the name of the One whom we follow. If we're not doing that, then that's not church.

Walking on Water

1. As a ministry team, what are some of the areas where you think you are already utilizing effective tools to encourage the spiritual formation of black Millennials?

2. What are some "sacred cows" in your ministry that may be hindering your work with engaging black Millennials?

3. What are some first steps your team can take this month toward engaging black Millennials based on the principles of this book?

Notes

1. Jennie Wilson, "Hold to God's Unchanging Hand," accessed April 1, 2017, http://www.hymnary.org/media/fetch/112503.

2. Aaron Earls, "Majority of American Churches Fall Below 100 in Worship Attendance," March 11, 2016, http://www.lifeway.com/pastors/2016/03/11/majority-of-american-churches-fall-below-100-in-worship-attendance/.

3. Johnson Oatman, "Lift Him Up," October 2, 2017, https://hymnary.org/text/how_to_reach_the_masses.

CHAPTER TEN

What's Next?

After reading through the information in this book and hearing the Valuable Voices of young black Millennial leaders on a wide range of topics, I imagine there may be some preachers, teachers, and leaders who are a bit overwhelmed. Most congregations are aware of the need to reach and retain Millennials for the benefit of their souls and for the survival of our congregations—but what I hope this book helps to display is that this can be a very costly effort. It can require making time to evaluate our processes and proclamation in ways that may be uncomfortable or that may cause radical departures from some of our norms. Some do not feel comfortable with the technological world and the way it challenges our privacy. Some may have even rejected some of the material in the book altogether based on theological or philosophical tensions. That's fine. The goal of this book was never to tell leaders what to think, but to share what black Millennials have shared with me in the study so that we can consider more effective ways to reach them and be effective partners in their spiritual formation journeys. For congregational leaders who have read and are ready to make steps toward implementing some of these suggestions, here are a few first steps to consider before launching out into the deep.

Mental Health Matters

One of the missing areas of conversation in my study surrounds mental health and the black church. Having worked with black Millennials as a Youth, College, and Young Adult minister for over a decade, I have observed that some of the quiet killers in this generation are depression and suicidal ideations. In recent years, I have sat with numerous students who have made attempts on their lives and many have silently dealt with depression for years. These are not young people who are rebels or recluses. In many cases, these are some of the church's "star" youth and young adults—actively participating and leading in the life of the church. These are young people who love God, worship earnestly, and seek to live out the tenets of the faith, but they are engaging in a fight for their lives mentally.

I am not a psychologist, but I do believe that the youngest of the Millennial generation and the generation to come behind them will continue to struggle in this area of mental health. Millennials have been called "the trophy kid" generation—where participation and participation alone are enough to be rewarded. This is the generation where not only does the winning basketball team get a trophy for their championship but each student gets one for playing on any team in the league. Many young Millennials grew up playing video games where the main characters would "die" if they did not successfully navigate a course—but the gaming consoles were also equipped with "reset" buttons that could be pushed to start the game over if things were not going the way that the player intended. One of the unintended consequences of these advances is the growth of a generation of young people, particularly the youngest Millennials, who do not know how to lose—how to work through defeat and disappointment and move forward.

Social media also has a huge role to play in this. While social media has opened incredible doors in connecting people groups and has expanded horizons in the area of platform building, social media also invites the world into what were once personal, if not private, conversations. The invention of "the Comments section," allowing any and all to provide commentary on everything one says or does in the social media world, has only heightened the anxieties and insecurities of this generation. This is the generation to first experience "cyberbullying," and while previous generations made similar childhood mistakes or missteps, technology has allowed this to become the first generation to act out their development on a worldwide stage—a stage that too many immaturely consent to crucify themselves on.

The church has a responsibility to be intentional and watchful as it relates to the mental health of both the Millennial parishioners we seek to engage and the leadership that engages them. This begins with our pulpit proclamations—ensuring that as we speak truth to power and boldly proclaim the Word of God, our rhetoric is not abusive to those whom we seek to minister to. In our excitement about the power of God, we must be careful about what we deem "crazy," about carelessly speaking about things that are making us "lose our minds." Ultimately there are young (and old) people in the congregation who are really losing their minds, depressed, and suicidal and the church must be responsible to operate in the knowledge of this reality. Moreover, the church must seek to break stigmas around black people seeking mental health treatment. Counselors or psychologists are not who people should speak with when they are "crazy," but rather they are ministering agents in partnership with God whom most of us could benefit from seeing with regularity. Invest in counseling for your ministry team if possible, as burnout and the weight of ministry can be a detriment to the mental health of church leaders.

Diversity and Dialogue

While my study gave us a pretty good understanding of some of the general values and desires of black Millennials, it is important to note that black Millennials are not monolithic. In fact, Millennials are the most diverse generation in American history. While this delineation is primarily a nod to the generation's racial diversity, it is important to note that black Millennials are diverse in other areas as well. Not all black Millennials are interested in hip hop music, BET, and basketball games. Not all black Millennials identify as Democrats or as political "liberals" (in fact, most participants in my study identified as "moderate"). Not all black Millennials are open and affirming as it relates to the LGBTQ community, as illustrated by the varying perspectives offered by Ms. Morris and Rev. Wright. It is therefore important for congregations not to make assumptions about the black Millennials in their congregations based on what they have heard or read, but to invest in getting to know them as individuals and tailoring programming to fit their needs.

In regards to theological diversity, theological formation is complicated business and has a lot to do with our training, the traditions in which we are raised, our socioeconomic make-up, and the bias we bring to our interpretation of Scripture. Throughout the book, I have sought not to impose my own theological beliefs and desires on readers, but rather to curate and expose readers to a variety of perspectives to consider through the findings of our study and the voices of emerging black faith leaders. I would, however, invite church leaders to create space for conversation around some of the doubts and concerns of black Millennials as described in this book. As I consult churches on ministry to Millennials, I often suggest that Christian educators create what I call "Theological Think Tanks." This is time when staff ministers, Sunday school teachers, and other Christian educators come together to caucus on specific theological issues. The senior pastor might send out an email two weeks before the think tank stating the topic of discussion and invite the Christian educators and clergy to build their arguments to support their positions. *What is our theological position on women in the church and society? What is our theological position and ethic as it relates to transgendered brothers and sisters in our congregation?* In most congregations, the theology of the house is set by the senior pastor, and while ultimately the senior pastor or ministry leader may make the final call on the stated position of the ministry following the think tank, this process forces Christian educators to be apologists and puts into conversation ideas and perspectives that the senior leadership may not have considered. The goal of this process is two-fold: first, to wrestle with concepts together to create well-thought-out arguments for the church's position, and second, to have all of the Christian educators leave the room "singing the same song" as they preach and teach within the church. Ultimately I believe that acknowledging diversity of thought and having serious and open dialogue is like "iron sharpening iron" and only makes our churches stronger.

Getting Buy-In

This book is full of implementable practices and strategies, some of which I present to ministry teams that I consult. At the end of most presentations, someone in the group will ask, "Rev. Mitchell, do you do *all* of this at your church?" The answer is always no. While having the information in this book as well as other resources is great, implementing them depends on the level of buy-in you have from the senior leadership (or denominational leadership) and the other "gatekeepers" or people who yield institutional power in your church (whether they have official titles or not). While I can say that most of the suggestions presented here have also been implemented in my current ministry context, there are some strategies that do not seem like the best fit for our culture—at least not right now. That's fine! If you're a minister or Christian educator who serves on a team and you are not the senior pastor or ministry leader, ultimately it is your job to serve God by working toward the vision that has been given to your senior leadership. Support this vision and implement what you can as you can.

I mention buy-in from gatekeepers because, in most congregations, the senior pastor is not the only gatekeeper or power broker with whom you have to work in tandem. I will never forget serving as a pastor for youth and young adults for a church in a rural area who had recently elected a new senior pastor. This was a church with great people who operated via traditional black Baptist church standards—for example, the Deacon Board led devotions and congregants wore suits and ties. In an effort to attract and engage the younger Millennials of the congregation, the senior pastor and I crafted a Youth Sunday experience, complete with relaxed attire, DJ, and Christian hip hop in the middle of worship. Talk about culture shock! During the first Youth Sunday, I was the "guest rapper" and performed one of the up-tempo Christian rap songs I had recorded in college. The energy was so high that I concluded the performance with a loud scream into the microphone, "He's my GOD!!!!" At the time, I felt that it was a hit!

I soon discovered that we probably would not be doing Youth Sunday that way anymore (at least, not with me rapping). While the ministry offering seemed to hit our target audience for that particular Sunday, it offended many of the gatekeepers and power brokers of the congregation who were experiencing this "hippity hop" in the middle of their sacred worship service for the first time. While the senior pastor and I had convened to plan and execute what we thought would be a great addition to the experience, I failed to realize that he was not the only gatekeeper to consider. In the end, the Deaconate was a powerful entity within that context. If we were going to radically alter worship to reach the black Millennials in our church, we needed the buy-in of the Deacon Board. Discern the powerbrokers and gatekeepers in your context and ensure that you have buy-in from them before you make any "radical" or culture-shifting changes.

Make the Investment

"For where your treasure is, there your heart will be also" (Matthew 6:21). In context, Matthew 6:21 is a call for Jesus' disciples to invest in the imperishable treasury of heaven—reminding them that the things they would invest in on earth are temporary. Yet Jesus' correlation between the heart and our areas of investment is true for both the eternal and the here and now. It does not take me long to identify whether or not a congregation is truly ready to do the hard work of engaging Millennials. Our ministry budgets and our calendars are normally clear indications of our priorities. In my estimation, reaching black Millennials requires time, talent, treasure, *and* training, and to effectively partner in the spiritual formation process of black Millennials, congregations must be willing to invest in these areas. This investment begins with people. As previously stated, we must invest in the lives and development of black Millennials without agenda or obligation—strictly out of Christian love. We have to champion some of the causes that are important to God and to them and help to provide them with resources to make it in this society. We must invest in black Millennials by preparing them for leadership roles—teaching them the tradition and culture of our congregations while empowering them to utilize their gifts and talents to lead and effectively serve. Invest in bringing in Millennial staffers and interns to help bolster and modernize our ministry work, as they are normally on the cutting edge of technological advancement and social engagement.

Invest in training for your leadership team. As mentioned previously, this is not simply investing in preaching conferences, but seeking spaces where creativity and innovation in worship and witness are being discussed and modeled. Invest in theological training for clergy and Christian educators as the church has opportunity. Go beyond the church world to learn about new trends and new technologies. While my pastor often reminds our team that the church does not have to take her cues from the world, it is good to see where the world is headed—particularly as it relates to technological advancement. Often churches are years behind in the use of technology that is normative for congregants outside of the sanctuary. It is important for churches to at least be aware of the digital tools and spaces where Millennials are engaged. Finally, invest in the changing technology because our digital landscape is of great importance to black Millennials. With the rapid improvements to personal consumer technology, it is no longer nearly as expensive to provide quality digital content—but *some* investment must be made financially.

Join the Conversation

One of the uncomfortable truths that the black church must wrestle with is that it is no longer the central hub for the black community—at least not for black Millennials. Moreover, the church must also see that it is not even the primary place where theological conversations are being held among Millennials. Before ever stepping into a church building, black Millennials are partaking in spiritual formation and being pastored through the music of Chance the Rapper, Kendrick Lamar, and Kanye West. They are receiving messaging about God and the worth of the church on television series like *Empire* and *Greenleaf*. These media forms should serve as refreshers for the church—displaying that black Millennials are not at all disinterested in the Divine but do need discipleship and direction in discerning the will and way of God. This is what the Christian church exists to do! It is up to congregations to be willing to engage in the conversations already being had about God in the public square and provide both encouragement and correction as only the church is uniquely equipped to do.

In closing, I leave readers with the words of Paul in Acts 17:22-25 (emphasis added): "People of Athens! I see that in every way you are very religious. For as I walked around and looked carefully at your objects of worship, I even found an altar with this inscription: TO AN UNKNOWN GOD. So you are ignorant of the very thing you worship—and this is what I am going to proclaim to you. The God who made the world and everything in it is the Lord of heaven and earth and does not live in temples built by human hands. And he is not served by human hands, as if he needed anything. Rather, he himself gives everyone life and breath and everything else." This is our call. Invest in the work, join the conversation, and lead this generation of Peters into the knowledge of this "unknown" God!

Walking on Water

1. What are some of the ways your ministry currently promotes mental health? What organizational steps can you take to help foster better mental health among your ministry team and congregants?

2. What are some of the diversities you see exhibited in the Millennials you engage? How does your programming reflect that diversity?

3. What investments can you make to ensure effective ministry to Millennials in your congregation?

4. What are some areas where God-related conversations are happening outside of the church? How can your congregation join and provide correction in those conversations?

Bibliography

Blumenthal, Eli. "Millennials drive spike in online shopping." *USA Today*, June 8, 2016. Accessed April 1, 2017. http://www.usatoday.com/story/money/2016/06/08/survey-more-than-half-purchases-made-online/85592598/

Douglas, Kelly Brown. *Sexuality and the Black Church: A Womanist Perspective*. New York: Orbis Books, 1999.

Earls, Aaron. "Majority of American Churches Fall Below 100 in Worship Attendance." March 11, 2016. Accessed April 1, 2017. http://www.lifeway.com/pastors/2016/03/11/majority-of-american-churches-fall-below-100-in-worship-attendance/

Eldridge, Lynn. "Understanding Anticipatory Grief: Why Am I Already Grieving?" Last modified July 27, 2017. Access April 1, 2017. https://www.verywell.com/understanding-anticipatory-grief-and-symptoms-2248855.

Fromm, Jeff and Christie Gartin. *Marketing to Millennials: Reach the Largest and Most Influential Generation of Consumers Ever*. New York: AMACOM, 2013.

Hamilton, Adam. *When Christians Get It Wrong*. Nashville: Abingdon Press, 2013. Kindle Edition.

Lightsey, Pamela R. *Our Lives Matter: A Womanist Queer Theology*. Oregon: Pickwick Publications, 2014.

McCarthy, Monsignor William. *The Conspiracy: An Innocent Priest*. Indiana: iUniverse Publishing, 2010.

Medicine Net Corporation. "Medical Definition of Anticipatory Grief," Accessed April 7, 2017. http://www.medicinenet.com/script/main/art.asp?articlekey=26258.

Oatman, Johnson. "Lift Him Up." October 2, 2017. https://

hymnary.org/text/how_to_reach_the_masses.

Oduah, Chika. "Are blacks abandoning Christianity for African faiths?" October 19, 2011. http://thegrio.com/2011/10/19/african-religions-gain-following-among-black-christians/.

Powe, F. Douglas, Jr. *New Wine, New Wineskins: How African American Congregations Can Reach New Generations*. Nashville: Abingdon Press, 2012. Kindle Edition.

Strauss, William and Neil Howe. *Millennials Rising: The Next Great Generation*. New York: Vintage Books, 2000. Kindle Edition.

Taylor, Paul. *The Next America: Boomers, Millennials, and the Looming Generational Showdown*. New York: Public Affairs, 2014. Kindle Edition.

West, Traci. *Wounds of The Spirit*. New York: New York University Press, 1999.

Wilson, Jennie. "Hold to God's Unchanging Hand." Accessed April 1, 2017. http://www.hymnary.org/media/fetch/112503.